CHRISTIAN HEROES: THEN & NOW

HUDSON TAYLOR

Obliged to Go

CHRISTIAN HEROES: Then & Now

HUDSON TAYLOR

Deep in the Heart of China

JANET & GEOFF BENGE

YWAM
PUBLISHING
P.O. BOX 55787   SEATTLE, WA 98155

YWAM Publishing is the publishing ministry of Youth With A Mission (YWAM), an international missionary organization of Christians from many denominations dedicated to presenting Jesus Christ to this generation. To this end, YWAM has focused its efforts in three main areas: (1) training and equipping believers for their part in fulfilling the Great Commission (Matthew 28:19), (2) personal evangelism, and (3) mercy ministry (medical and relief work).

For a free catalog of books and materials, call (425) 771-1153 or (800) 922-2143. Visit us online at www.ywampublishing.com.

Hudson Taylor: Deep in the Heart of China
Copyright © 1998 by YWAM Publishing

Published by YWAM Publishing
a ministry of Youth With A Mission
P.O. Box 55787, Seattle, WA 98155-0787

ISBN-13: 978-1-57658-016-5
ISBN-10: 1-57658-016-4

Ninth printing 2016

Printed in the United States of America

Christian Heroes: Then & Now

Available in paperback, e-book, and audiobook formats. Unit study curriculum guides are available for select biographies.

www.HeroesThenAndNow.com

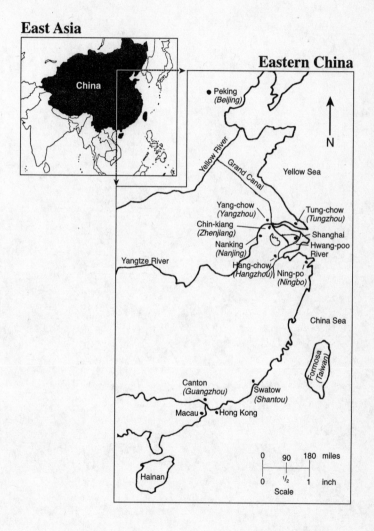

East Asia

China

Eastern China

Peking
(Beijing)

Yellow River

Grand Canal

Yellow Sea

N

Yang-chow
(Yangzhou)

Tung-chow
(Tungzhou)

Chin-kiang
(Zhenjiang)

Shanghai

Hwang-poo
River

Nanking
(Nanjing)

Yangtze River

Hang-chow
(Hangzhou)

Ning-po
(Ningbo)

China Sea

Formosa
(Taiwan)

Canton
(Guangzhou)

Swatow
(Shantou)

Macau

Hong Kong

Hainan

0   90   180   miles

0   ½   1   inch

Scale

Contents

Chapter 1

Dangerous Light

Captain Morris gripped the wheel of the *Dumfries*, a 470-ton wooden sailing ship, as he barked orders at his twenty-three man crew. In his cabin below deck, the ship's only passenger, Hudson Taylor, sat writing in his journal. The short, young Englishman with blond hair and blue eyes was on his way to be a missionary in China. Busy writing, he didn't know that the ship was headed into a storm, though he did notice that the lantern in his cabin was beginning to swing more than it had been.

On deck, the barometric pressure was dropping steadily. Low pressure meant high winds, and high winds meant rough sea. Waves were beginning to break across the bow of the ship. With each one, the

Dumfries rolled from side to side, shuddering and creaking. The stronger the wind grew, the more worried Captain Morris became. Despite all his efforts, his ship was at the mercy of the current and the howling wind. And worse, they were just four days out of Liverpool and not yet in the open waters of the Atlantic Ocean. They were still in the Irish Sea, close to the jagged, rocky outcrops of the Welsh coastline. Now, tossed to and fro by the wind and the ocean current, those rocks were perilously close.

By late afternoon, the waves were mountainous, and the *Dumfries* creaked as it lurched. Hudson Taylor made his way cautiously up on deck. The color of the sky matched the bruises he'd gotten while being tossed around in his cabin. Ocean spray stung like tiny shards of glass as it whipped at his face.

Captain Morris clung to the ship's large wooden wheel, turning it first one way and then the other, trying to get the *Dumfries* to respond. He glanced at Hudson, not once slackening his grip.

"Unless God helps us, there is no hope," he yelled.

"How far are we from the Welsh Coast?" Hudson shouted back.

"Fifteen or sixteen miles, and we're drifting fast."

As Captain Morris spoke, a huge wave hurled itself against the ship. Frothing foam driven by the wind filled the air, and water surged across the deck, tossing barrels and pieces of lumber around as though they weighed nothing. Hudson decided he would be safer down in his cabin. As he left the deck, he surveyed the scene before heading below. *Unless God works miraculously on our behalf, a few broken timbers will be all that's left of us and our ship by morning,* he thought, unsure of what lay ahead.

In the darkness below deck, many of the *Dumfries'* crew huddled together in the mess room. The ship was pitching and rolling so heavily—now falling forward, now rocking from side to side, now falling *and* rocking—that Hudson had to crawl on his hands and knees down the passage to his cabin in the ship's stern. The cabin door swung wildly on its hinges, but he managed to secure it behind him as he collapsed inside. He rolled onto his bunk, alone in the dark, hearing only the smash of the waves against the ship's side and the ship's shuddering reply. Each swell nearly threw him from his bunk.

He tried to sleep, but it was no use. The fury of the storm only grew, until the ship was being tossed so wildly that Hudson could not remain in his bunk. He made his way back up on deck. Captain Morris still stood resolutely at the wheel. But Hudson noticed something different this time. He could see a lighthouse close to the leeward side of the ship.

"The Holyhead Lighthouse," Captain Morris yelled to Hudson. "We're heading straight for it."

"How long do we have?" Hudson bellowed back over the howl of the wind.

"Two hours at the most," was the captain's grim reply.

Hudson could think of nothing else to say. It was over. Captain Morris had done everything he could to save his ship, but nothing had worked. It was only a matter of time before the *Dumfries* would smash into the rocks. Tears joined the salty trail of sea spray that streaked down Hudson's cheeks.

Thoughts of family flooded Hudson's mind as he made his way back below deck. He could see the faces of his mother and father and his sisters Amelia and Louisa. How would they cope with his death? It was not supposed to end this way. Had God saved him from malignant fever and certain death only to let him drown in the Irish Sea? He thought about his body. Would it sink to the bottom or wash up on shore? Just in case it washed up, he took out his pocketbook and, despite the fierce, unpredictable movements of the *Dumfries*, managed to write his name and address in large letters inside the cover. He slipped the book inside his undershirt. Now, if his body washed up, his family would know he'd been identified and properly buried.

Next he began looking for something that would float, something he could cling to when the *Dumfries* sank. As he looked, he realized that floating was less of a problem than avoiding being smashed against the rocks by the raging sea. But there was nothing he could do about that; he would just have to take his chances. Finally he settled on a cane hamper as a life preserver. It would surely float, and it was easy to cling to. Inside the hamper he put a little food, a change of clothes, some rope, and his surgical tools. With this unlikely lifesaving kit tucked under his arm, he once again made his way to the deck. A hatchway door had been ripped from its hinges, and water was now pouring in below deck through the hatch. Several crew members were scrambling to cover the gaping hole with a piece of torn sail and some lumber.

On deck, Captain Morris was still standing at the *Dumfries'* wheel, where he had been standing for the past twenty-four hours. Frothing water swirled around his legs as wave after wave washed violently over the ship's railing.

Hudson gripped the railing and pulled himself towards the captain. Above him, the halyards whipped against the mast. Captain Morris was trying to get the *Dumfries* to tack, zigzagging the ship first one way and then the other, to get away from the rocks. But it was no use. The wind was just too strong, and the ship still would not respond. Yard by yard they were being pushed toward Holyhead Lighthouse and the ship-smashing rocks of the Welsh coast.

The lighthouse beam passed rhythmically, eerily, over the *Dumfries'* bow. It was the kind of light no sailor ever wanted to see this close.

Knowing he was about to lose his ship, Captain Morris checked his instruments one last time. The barometer revealed that the pressure was beginning to rise, but not fast enough to be of any use to them. Then he checked the wind gauge. Suddenly, he shouted. "The wind has shifted," he cried. "Only two points mind you, but enough that we might be able to clear the rocks."

He barked orders to his crew, who scurried up from below deck to carry them out. They pulled at the halyards with all their might to set the sails to take advantage of the wind shift. Captain Morris skillfully adjusted the *Dumfries'* wheel, and this time the ship began to respond. Instead of being swept closer to the rocks, it began to inch away from them. Inches turned to feet, and feet into yards, and soon the *Dumfries* was headed back out into the Irish Sea. Everyone on board let out a loud cry. They were safe!

None was more surprised or happy than Hudson Taylor. He was not going to drown after all. He was going to make it to China. He smiled to himself. Four days out of England and he'd already had his first sea adventure. If the junior clerks at the Barnsley Bank could see him now!

Chapter 2

A Mother's Prayer

The boys at work were right, Hudson Taylor thought to himself, as his father continued to read. *I live the most boring life in the whole of Barnsley, probably in the whole of England. Why do I have to be stuck here listening to this morning after morning?* He was listening to his father read from the Bible. It followed right on from the Bible reading the night before, but Hudson hadn't been listening then, either. He glanced around at his two younger sisters, Amelia and Louisa. They were paying perfect attention, their blonde ringlets of hair hung still, and there was a serious expression on both of their faces. His mother sat on the other side of the table, nodding her head slowly in agreement as Mr. Taylor read. *How boring!*

Hudson's mind drifted back to when he had started working at the bank. How naive he'd been, thinking the other junior clerks would be impressed by the fact that in 1791 his grandfather had built the town's first Methodist chapel on Pinfold Hill. Or that his family had attended the church every single Sunday since then. Instead of being impressed with his family's history, his Bible knowledge, and the fact he could even read the Bible in Latin, his coworkers had laughed at his childish faith and began challenging everything he'd always *presumed* to be correct about his religion.

"Presumed," that *was* the right word. When he'd been told about Jesus and the Christian faith, he'd presumed the person was telling him the truth. But was he? What if there was no real truth? What if people just believed because other people told them to believe? And what about Christians being hypocrites? Hudson's coworkers were always throwing that one up. Were they right? Hudson could certainly think of a few people at church who easily fit the category. His head swirled with thoughts that had never even crossed his mind until he'd started working at the bank nine months earlier. His experiences were so narrow, his upbringing sheltered, and his life downright boring. By comparison, the lives of the young men he worked with seemed filled with the promise of adventure. While they were making the most of life, he, a sixteen-year-old no less, was stuck at home sitting at the table with his twelve- and eight-year-old sisters, listening to his father drone on and on.

Eventually, Mr. Taylor clapped the Bible shut and said a final prayer. Then he turned to Hudson. "Come downstairs before you go to work today, I want to take a look at those eyes of yours."

Hudson nodded reluctantly. His father didn't miss a thing. Hudson's eyes had been hurting a lot lately, especially when he tried to balance the ledgers at the bank. But he hadn't wanted to tell his father about the problem because deep down he had a suspicion that his eye problem had something to do with the gas lamps at the bank. And since working at the bank was his escape from boredom, he didn't want sore eyes to come between him and this newfound freedom.

Hudson descended the stairs from the family living area to the pharmacy below. The familiar smell of herbs and potions greeted him as he stepped into his father's world of bottles and pill boxes. Mr. Taylor beckoned for him to come and sit down on the stool in the back room. This was where he examined his customers' ailments. He lifted Hudson's eyelids and peered into one eye and then the other through a magnifying glass. He asked questions. How long had they been hurting? Was it worse in the morning or at night?

Finally, the diagnosis was made. Both of Hudson's eyes were badly inflamed—a serious problem that could make him blind. The only hope for a full recovery was total rest. Hudson sat stunned. He knew it had been too good to last. There would be no more working at the bank, no more laughing with the other junior clerks. Instead, he'd be stuck at home all day long being cared for by his mother and sisters. It was so unfair, but what did he expect? It had been this way all his life. Every time something started to go right for him, he would get sick. And ever since his younger brother William and then his baby brother Theodore had died, his parents had become extra cautious. Life already seemed totally boring, but Hudson had a feeling it was going to get a whole lot worse in the weeks ahead.

As he lay in his darkened bedroom, all thought of adventure drained from his mind. The water dripping from the wet rags pressed against his eyes mingled with the tears of self-pity that ran across his cheeks. He could see his life stretched out before him, and it wasn't a happy sight. As the only son, he would one day own the pharmacy. One thing would be different, though, Hudson promised himself. There would be no more Bible reading each morning when he was running things. And he wouldn't be praying with his children either. If nothing else, his time at the bank had shown him just how old-fashioned these religious ideas were.

Hudson made a slow recovery, and when his eyes had healed sufficiently, he began working with his father. He was glad to be up and about again. And he was glad that the pain was gone from his eyes. But now that he was better, he resented having to go to church again with the family. Mr. Taylor was used to being obeyed by his children, and he made sure Hudson joined them each Sunday. But Mrs. Taylor could see the frustration building in her son. She worried about him. And she prayed for him every day.

Two years passed, and while Hudson had settled into the routine of working with his father in the pharmacy, he couldn't shake his feelings of frustration. All the while, Mrs. Taylor kept on praying for him.

Sometimes actions carried out by different people in different places at different times can meet together in one moment and completely change the course of a life. Such a moment happened to Hudson Taylor in June 1849, two years after leaving the bank.

The first action was taken by his sister Amelia, who was now fourteen. She looked up to her older brother and had been worried for some time about how he had drifted away from God. She decided to do something about it. In her diary she made a note that she would pray for Hudson three times a day until he found peace with God. And, true to her word, she prayed for him faithfully.

The second event happened a month later when Mrs. Taylor went to spend several weeks visiting her sister. While she was away she actually had some spare time, something she never seemed to have at home, attending to the needs of her busy household. So she decided to spend an afternoon praying for Hudson.

On that same afternoon, back at home, Hudson was feeling particularly bored. He knew, though, that if he didn't look busy his little sister Louisa would pester him to play paper dolls with her, or worse, his father would find some chore for him to do. So Hudson decided to take a good book to his favorite hideaway. But he couldn't seem to find anything that interested him on the bookshelf; he'd read all the good books until he knew passages from many of them by heart. It was then that he spotted a religious booklet he had not seen before. His father was always collecting them and giving them to his customers. Hudson smiled to himself as he took the book off the shelf. He had figured out how these booklets worked a long time ago. The first half was always an exciting story to get people's interest, and then the second half was a Gospel message. Hudson had heard enough Gospel messages already in his lifetime, so he promised himself he would read only the first half.

With the book tucked firmly under his arm, and keeping an eye out in case Louisa discovered his hideaway, he hurried to the old warehouse at the back of their property and settled down to read.

Forty-five miles away at her sister's house, Hudson's mother was praying fervently for him. After several hours of praying she felt a peace come over her. Somewhere deep inside she knew God had answered her prayers. She didn't know how it happened, but she was certain her son had become a Christian.

And amazingly, he had. Hudson had begun reading the story in the booklet, and it had interested him so much that he'd forgotten all about his promise to read only the first half of the book. Before he knew it, he had read the Gospel part as well. As he read, a phrase seemed to jump out at him. "The finished work of Christ," the booklet said, and Hudson couldn't seem to get that phrase out of his mind. He thought about it at great length. If it was a finished work, then there was nothing he could do but accept that finished work. And so, there in his hideaway in the old warehouse, Hudson Taylor invited Jesus Christ to come into his life.

Hudson left the warehouse a new person; the struggle that had raged on inside him for so long was finally settled. For the first time since starting work at the bank nearly three years earlier, he felt at peace inside.

He wanted his mother to be the first one to know, and since she was not yet back from visiting her sister, he said nothing to anyone else about what had happened.

A few days went by, and Amelia and Louisa watched Hudson with fascination. Something about him was different. Finally Amelia asked him what had happened, and Hudson confided in her that he had become a Christian. He explained that he had not told her sooner because he wanted their mother to be the first to know, and so he swore Amelia to secrecy.

It was two weeks before Mrs. Taylor returned

from visiting her sister. Hudson could hardly wait to see her face and tell her the good news. Finally he heard her footsteps on the stairway. He flung open the door and wrapped his arms around his mother. When he had nearly squeezed the life from her, he let her go and announced that he had some wonderful news for her. Mrs. Taylor smiled broadly. "I already know what you have to tell me," she said, nodding. "You have made your peace with God, and I have been rejoicing in that knowledge for two weeks."

Hudson stepped back, stunned. Only one person in the world knew of his conversion, and that was Amelia. Had she written to their mother? "How did you know?" he asked. "Did Amelia break her promise? She said she wouldn't tell anyone."

Mrs. Taylor laughed. "No, I have not heard it from any earthly source. I was praying for you while I was away, and as I prayed, the Holy Spirit made it known to me that He had claimed you." Hudson was both relieved that his sister hadn't lied to him and shocked by how sure his mother had been of his conversion.

As they continued their conversation, Hudson learned that his mother had been praying at the exact moment he had come to understand the real meaning of being a Christian.

Several days later, Hudson picked up what he thought was his notebook to check for something he had written. Just as he opened it, he realized he'd picked up Amelia's notebook by mistake. But before he could close it, a passage with his name in it caught his eye. The passage was her diary entry, and in it she promised to pray for him three times a day until he had become a Christian. It was dated exactly one month before he picked up the booklet and read it in his hideaway.

Hudson was amazed. God really did answer prayer. He found himself wondering what would happen next in this new world of faith he had entered.

Chapter 3

One Single Word

Now that Hudson was a believer, he couldn't wait for Sundays at the Methodist chapel on Pinfold Hill. Bible reading was no longer boring. Every time the Bible was read now, words jumped out at him. And what had once been dull, dry sermons were filled with new meaning. And while he knew he was too young to lead the church Bible class, or any other church activity for that matter, he also knew that somewhere there was something he could do for God.

Finally one day, he and Amelia had an idea. They decided to skip the Sunday evening service, which they loved, and instead spend the time visiting homes in the poorest areas of Barnsley. As they went, they would hand out tracts, invite people to church, and tell them about God's love and concern for them. Amelia and Hudson grew very close during this time as they planned and prayed together for their Sunday visits. They felt happy, and neither of them could see any reason why their visiting could not continue indefinitely. Mr. and Mrs. Taylor, however, had other plans.

Amelia was now fourteen years old, and her parents had been looking for a good school for her to attend. After much searching they decided to send their daughter to the boarding school run by Aunt Hodson, Mrs. Taylor's sister, at Barton-upon-Humber, forty-five miles away. Amelia would be able to come back and visit during vacations, and she would be in good hands with her aunt.

Meanwhile, Aunt Hodson had also been wondering what to do with her son John. He was finished with school and needed a job. So it was decided that in return for Amelia's attending school in Barton-upon-Humber, John would come and live with the Taylor family and be an apprentice pharmacist to Mr. Taylor. It was to be a straight swap of children and would not cost either family a penny, except for the train fare home at vacation time.

It all seemed to work out perfectly, except for a few *minor* details. Hudson lost his best friend and prayer partner and in exchange got a constant companion who reminded him of the junior clerks at the bank. John never seemed to take anything seriously, especially Hudson's need for privacy. Amelia and Louisa had always shared a bedroom, while Hudson had his own. Now things were different. Hudson's personal belongings had been moved aside, and a second bed moved into the room. And if that weren't enough, John talked endlessly about things that did not interest Hudson. He would even interrupt Hudson while he was praying or reading his Bible to tell him a joke. It was a very difficult time. And despite the presence of John in his bedroom, Hudson felt lonely. To him, John seemed an unfair exchange for Amelia.

Through it all, Hudson continued to pray and read his Bible. It was during this time that he heard God speak the one word that would be the focal point of every major decision he would make for the rest of his life. One single word—*China*.

One day Hudson was praying and telling God how his life seemed so unfocused and frustrating. He'd tried to do the right thing, but it was so difficult to live a godly life, especially with John breathing down his neck all the time. Finally, in desperation, Hudson told God that if He would break the power of sin in his life he would do anything God asked him to do, go anywhere God asked him to go, and speak to anyone God asked him to speak to. As Hudson prayed his prayer out loud, great peace came over him. Later he wrote about it: "Never shall I forget the feeling that came over me then. Words can never describe it. I felt I was in the presence of God....Something seemed to say 'Your prayer is answered, your conditions are accepted.' And from that time the conviction never left me that I was called to China."

In the same way that his father's magnifying glass focused sunlight into a narrow band of powerful light, so Hudson's life began to focus on China.

Every decision and every activity became valuable only if it moved him towards his goal. This focus on China took several forms. First, he realized he would need all the academic training he could get. He had been taught at home most of his life because he wasn't always strong enough to attend school, so he was used to setting his own course of study.

In a letter to Amelia he explained why he had begun getting up at 5 A.M. to study: "I must study if I mean to go to China. I am fully decided to go, and am making every preparation I can. I intend to rub up on [improve] my Latin, to learn Greek and the rudiments of Hebrew, and to get as much general information as possible."

Second, he needed to toughen up his body. His mother had always fussed over him because he was so often sick. She made sure he sat where there was no draft, ate wholesome food, and was careful to wrap up warm on cold winter days when he went out to deliver medicines. But all of this fussing made Hudson wonder how he would ever survive in China, not to mention the dangerous sea voyage to get there. There was nothing else for it but to toughen up! He started with a strenuous exercise program outside in the cold. His mother found it difficult to look out the window and see him working so hard on frosty mornings. She worried that he would catch pneumonia.

Hudson also got rid of his feather bed and began sleeping on bare boards. He gave away many things that were not "essential" to his daily life. *When I get to China,* he told himself, *my body must be ready.*

Third, Hudson had to find some way to learn the Chinese language. Of course, he didn't know anyone who had been to China, much less spoke Chinese, so there was no way he could learn how the language sounded. But he could learn what it looked like written down. It so happened that someone had given him a copy of the Gospel of Luke in Chinese. There was just one catch: there was no translation or dictionary to go with it. The chapter and verse numbers were in English as well as Chinese, however. Hudson managed to persuade John to help him, and together they set about unraveling the puzzle of the Chinese language.

The traditional Chinese language is written in pictographic form. That means that a picture represents an idea. A picture of the sun and moon together is translated as the word *bright.* (In English, of course, we use letters to stand for the actual sounds we make. This means English is a phonetically written language.) Even though there were many languages and dialects spoken in China, everyone was able to look at the picture of the sun and the moon and know it meant bright, no matter how the word was actually said. This made learning to write Chinese a very valuable skill.

This is how Hudson and John worked out what the pictograms meant: They would pick a word in English and then find it in a verse in an English copy of the Gospel of Luke. If they were looking at the word *salvation* they might identify Luke chapter 2, verse 30: "For mine eyes have seen thy salvation." Then they would use an English concordance to find ten or twelve other verses in Luke that had the word *salvation* in them, such as Luke chapter 3 verse 6: "All flesh shall see the salvation of God," and Luke chapter 19 verse 19: "Today salvation has come to this house." Then came the tricky part. They would then find the same verses in the Chinese Gospel of Luke and write them out one under the other. They then searched for the pictogram that appeared in *all* the Chinese verses. Finally they searched the entire Gospel in Chinese, looking for more verses with the same pictogram in them. If, in every instance, they found the pictograph to be where the English word could be found, they would enter it into a notebook in pencil.

Later, if they did not find a single place where that pictogram seemed to mean something else, they would trace the pictogram in ink.

Slowly, one word at a time, they identified and memorized the Chinese characters, until Hudson could read and write over 500 of them.

Not only did Hudson need to know the Chinese language, but also he realized that he needed to know more about China itself, particularly beyond the coastal areas. In 1850 it was not easy to find out much about China. The Chinese people were very good at keeping secrets, since they did not want foreigners, or "white barbarians," as they called them, to influence their way of life. This was partly because of the Opium War, in which the English humiliated the Chinese people. The Chinese were not about to forgive the English for that humiliation.

The Opium War had begun in 1839, when Hudson was seven years old. It was fought over trade rights between England and China. English people wanted many things that the Chinese had to sell: silk, spices, tea, and porcelain china, to name a few. The Chinese, though, didn't want anything the English had to sell except for a little silver. This led to a huge trade imbalance. The English soon owed the Chinese lots of money, and they were frustrated that the Chinese didn't want to buy things from them to even out how much they owed. So they set about trying to come up with something the Chinese did want.

Unfortunately, some English officials came up with a very clever but very horrible plan. They would sell the Chinese people a drug called opium, a drug that was very addictive so they would need to buy more and more of it. Opium came from special poppies that grew in India, a country the British had already overrun and made part of their empire. Before the Chinese government knew what was happening, 40,000 cases of the drug were being brought into China each year, causing thousands and thousands of Chinese people to become addicted to opium. It was a nightmare for the Chinese. People lay in the streets begging for opium, high officials became addicted and made foolish decisions, and even the emperor's own son died from an overdose of the drug.

No matter how much it angered the British, the emperor decided they had to be stopped. He declared a ban on the import of opium. The English, of course, were not ready to give up their new trading item, and so war began. It was a war that didn't take the English long to win. Even though China had invented gunpowder many centuries before, it was the British who knew how to use it in cannons and guns. The Chinese were hopelessly outgunned by their invaders and were defeated in 1842. They were forced to sign the Treaty of Nanking. It was a very unequal treaty. But then, the British had won, and the Chinese had lost. As one condition for ending the bombardment of China, the emperor had to agree to give the island of Hong Kong to the British and to open up five cities along the coast as places for foreigners to live and trade. But the treaty said nothing about opium imports. The Chinese had lost the real battle they had set out to win, the right to keep opium out of their country.

The Chinese were very bitter about this foreign interference, and while they tolerated traders and a few missionaries in the "treaty ports," as they were called, they would not let missionaries, or any foreign "barbarians," venture into the inland areas.

This was still the basic state of affairs between the two countries when Hudson began to focus his attention on China. Hudson knew the Chinese would not welcome him or the message he brought. Yet the tracts he got from the Chinese Evangelization Society in London inspired him. There was such an enormous number of people in China who had never heard about Jesus Christ. Hudson read and reread the tracts, trying to grasp the numbers of people they talked about. He studied the map until he worked out that Great Britain would fit into China about forty times. One tract estimated the number of people in China to be 400 million. It seemed almost too big a number to be true.

About this time, Hudson heard that the local Congregational minister had a good book on China called *China, Its State and Prospects*, by Walter Medhurst. He knew that Medhurst had printed copies of the Bible in Chinese and disguised himself as a native in order to smuggle them up the rivers into Inland China. Hudson could hardly wait to read the book and learn about Medhurst's adventures.

"May I borrow your copy of Walter Medhurst's book?" Hudson politely asked the Congregational minister.

"Certainly," said the minister. "But I am curious as to what a pharmacist's son wants with such a book."

"I intend to be a missionary in China, sir," Hudson replied. "I need to find out as much about the place as I possibly can, and this book has been recommended to me."

"And how are you going to pay for your trip and support yourself once you get to China?" The minister inquired.

"Like the disciples in the New Testament who took nothing when Jesus sent them to minister to people, I, too, will trust God to supply all my needs," Hudson said confidently.

The minister smiled. "I have some advice for you, young man," he said in a kind voice, putting his hand on Hudson's shoulder. "As you grow older you will become wiser. You will see that such an idea was fine in the days when Christ Himself was on earth, but not now."

Hudson was surprised to hear words like this from a man of God, but he was not discouraged. Medhurst's book was too exciting! It described rice paddy-covered plains, walled cities, enormous mountain ranges, yak trips, and river voyages. Hudson read it from cover to cover several times. And he took some advice, not from the Congregational minister, but from the book itself. Medhurst strongly urged potential missionaries to get medical training before they arrived in China. Something clicked in Hudson when he read this. Now he had another focus in his training for China: Yes, he would go to China, but with medical training! Of course, the question was, how to get such training?

Before he could find an answer to the question, it was time for Amelia to come home for the summer vacation. Eighteen-year-old Hudson couldn't wait to share his new direction with his sister.

When Amelia arrived home, she did not come alone. She brought with her the school's music teacher, Marianne Vaughan. Marianne was lively and funny, pretty and talented. She played the piano and sang for them. Hudson was hooked! He couldn't believe how perfect she was. He reasoned that God had brought Marianne into his life so he would have a wife to go with him to China. It all fitted so perfectly. He imagined them as a team, the first missionaries ever to set foot in a far-off Chinese village. He would preach and give medical advice while Marianne taught the children and led singing.

The three of them spent a wonderful summer together horseback riding, singing, and laughing. By the time Marianne and Amelia boarded the train for Barton-upon-Humber and the boarding school, Hudson felt sure he had spent the most wonderful summer of his life with his future wife.

After they had gone, he still had to work out how to get medical training. The obvious place to go was London. But it was so expensive to live there. He would have to work full time just to pay for his food, accommodations, and school fees, leaving him no time to actually attend medical school. No matter how hard he tried, he couldn't seem to come up with a solution that worked. Fortunately for him, his mother's other sister, Aunt Hannah, who lived in Hull, came up with an idea. Her brother-in-law, Robert Hardey, was a well-respected doctor in Hull, and he was looking for an assistant. In exchange for room and board and a small wage, as well as access to the classes Doctor Hardey taught at a local medical school, would Hudson be willing to become the doctor's assistant?

It was a question Hudson didn't need to be asked more than once. On his nineteenth birthday he boarded a train headed for Hull, fifty miles away, and, in so doing, took another step closer to China.

Chapter 4

The Opportunity of a Lifetime

Everything was working out better than Hudson had hoped. Dr. Hardey was a well-respected doctor and a good Christian man. He was kind and considerate. He saw potential in Hudson and gave him a lot of responsibility. And although there was much to learn, Hudson found that in many ways he was well prepared for his new duties.

One duty was the accounting; his days as a junior clerk at the bank had provided him with a basic understanding of bookkeeping. He also had to recommend and dispense medicines; five years working under his father's watchful eye had taught him a lot about medicines, not to mention the care his father had insisted he take when mixing them. And he had to write notes and prescriptions, all in

Latin, the language of medicine in nineteenth-century England. His father had taught him Latin, too.

Life quickly fell into a pleasant rhythm for Hudson. He spent most of his spare time studying for the classes that Doctor Hardey taught at Hull Medical School. On Sundays he would attend church and either visit his Aunt Hannah and Uncle Richard or take the slightly longer trip to Barton-upon-Humber to spend the afternoon with Marianne and Amelia.

On one such visit, Hudson could hardly wait to show Marianne and Amelia an article he had read in *The Gleaner*, a magazine put out by the Chinese Evangelization Society. The article was about a German man named Wilhelm Lobscheid, who had been to Inland China. Lobscheid was going to hold a public meeting in London to tell people about his experiences in China. Hudson told Marianne and Amelia all about what he had read. As he did so, Amelia's eyes lit up with excitement. But to his surprise, Marianne seemed bored by it all. "Do you have to go to China to serve God? Couldn't you become a doctor and do church work here?" she finally asked him.

Her question caught Hudson off guard. A puzzled look spread across his face. *How many times had he explained to her about how he felt called to China? How could they ever get married if she didn't share that same calling?* Hudson didn't answer Marianne's question; instead he resolved in his heart that he would trust God to change the way she felt about China.

Amelia burst in with her own question for Hudson. "Do you intend to go to London to hear Mr. Lobscheid?" When he said that he did, Amelia began to question him more closely. How would he pay for the ticket to get there? Did he have anywhere to stay? Would Dr. Hardey allow him the time off?

Hudson didn't have the answers to all her questions, but somehow he knew he would find a way to meet this man who had firsthand experience of China.

Not long after, huge posters began appearing all over Hull and in every other city in England. "Come to the Great Exhibition of Industry of All Nations," the posters read. But it was the line of text under this that got Hudson's heart racing with excitement. "The Opportunity of a Lifetime—Special Excursion Fares to London Available." What was so exciting was that the opening of the Great Exhibit was at the same time as Lobscheid's talk in London. The special train fares might be cheap enough for him to get to London after all.

It turned out that the fares were even cheaper than Hudson had hoped. Queen Victoria wanted as many of her subjects as possible to see the amazing show. This "Great Exhibition" was the first of its kind and was the brainchild of Prince Albert, Queen Victoria's husband. The prince had imagined a great gathering of people, where exhibitors from all over the world could bring the latest technology from their countries to display. Prince Albert ordered a huge glass and iron-framed building to be built for the exhibition. When the building was completed, it was named the Crystal Palace.

Over 13,000 exhibitors had set up displays in the huge building, and now it was time for as many people as possible to see the exhibits. To help get people to London for the Great Exhibition, cheap train fares—cheap enough that Hudson could buy two of them—were being offered. Hudson intended to use one train fare to get himself to London, and the other he was going to give to Amelia as a sixteenth birthday present.

Hudson arranged with Dr. Hardey for some time off and set out on his first trip to London. His mind whirled with all the possibilities that lay ahead in London. He would get to talk to a real missionary from China; meet Mr. Pearse, the secretary of the Chinese Evangelization Society, whom he had begun keeping in touch with by letter; and see the most fascinating plants, animals, and inventions from all over the world. He would also get to spend time with Amelia, who was thrilled to be able to go with him on the trip. Any one of these things would have made him happy; getting to do all of them together was almost too good to be true.

Villages, wooded glades, and fields rolled by outside the train, but Hudson's mind was elsewhere. He was imagining himself meeting Wilhelm Lobscheid. He was going to tell Lobscheid all about his preparations for China. Hudson hoped Mr. Lobscheid would return the favor by giving him some special insights, especially pointing out the next step for him to take in preparing for China.

The first few days in London were thrilling for Hudson and Amelia. Huge crowds were everywhere. The streets were jammed with wagons, carts, and stagecoaches. One of their favorite things to do was ride the horse-drawn omnibus. On many of the omnibuses, passengers were allowed to sit in seats on the roof. And that's where Amelia and Hudson loved to sit and enjoy the bird's-eye view of all the activity of London.

And if the sights of London were not enough, the Great Exhibition truly amazed them. It had been billed as the most unforgettable event of the nineteenth century, and the billing was not wrong! Hudson and Amelia walked up and down all eight miles of aisles looking at the exhibits. It was an amazing display of the practical and the improbable. There were many technological "firsts": the first rotary digger, the first baby carriage, the first revolver. It was also the first time English people got to see a new product from India called rubber. An American company demonstrated a machine that made ice, while another company demonstrated an alarm clock that woke the sleeper by turning the bed over! Even the Crystal Palace itself was unlike anything people had seen before. It was a huge, rectangular building that covered twenty-five acres of Hyde Park, right in the middle of London. It was made entirely of glass and iron and had room enough within it for twenty-foot fountains, potted palm trees, and elephants to roam around. It was said that the whole building had been designed in such a way that it could be dismantled and put together again on another site once the exhibit was over. Amelia and Hudson were amazed by all the new things they saw.

Yet despite the amazing sights of London and the Great Exhibition, Sunday was what they had come for, and finally Sunday arrived. Mr. Pearse met them and took them to a church in Tottenham to hear Wilhelm Lobscheid speak. During the gathering, Hudson had time to study Lobscheid, a tall, bony man with olive skin and a slight red tinge to his thick, dark hair. When Lobscheid spoke of China, his face lit up.

Finally the gathering drew to a close, and Hudson eagerly waited for the moment when he would meet Wilhelm Lobscheid face to face. The moment soon arrived. Mr. Pearse introduced Hudson, who shook hands with Lobscheid. Hudson immediately began telling all about how God had called him to China and the preparations he was making. Wilhelm Lobscheid smiled as he listened, and then he began to laugh out loud. Surprised, Hudson stopped what he was saying mid-sentence. "Why, you will never do for China," Lobscheid said, staring hard at Hudson's fair hair and blue eyes. "They call me 'red-headed devil,'" he laughed. "They would run from you and your blonde hair in terror! You could never get the Chinese to listen to you."

Hudson was speechless. He had spent so much time wondering and planning how he would adjust to the Chinese that he had never given any thought to how the Chinese would adjust to him! Yet he knew God had called him, and no matter how much this veteran missionary laughed, that was the promise he was going to cling to. So he looked into Lobscheid's eyes and, trying to hide his disappointment, said, "It is God who has called me to China, and He knows the color of my hair and eyes." Lobscheid just laughed louder.

Despite his obvious disappointment, the day turned out to be a good one for Hudson. He'd had a wonderful time getting to know Mr. Pearse better, and he had also been introduced to a number of members from the Chinese Evangelization Society. Both he and Amelia were wholeheartedly welcomed into this group of people whose desire was to see the gospel preached throughout China. And from that meeting, many friendships were begun— friendships that would last throughout Hudson's lifetime.

Hudson returned to Hull, where soon after, Dr. Hardey announced that his bedroom was needed for a family member. He was sorry, but Hudson would have to find somewhere else to live. So Hudson moved in with Aunt Hannah and Uncle Richard.

After the move, Hudson found life even easier for him than it had been with Dr. Hardey. His aunt and uncle had no children of their own, so they spoiled him. Aunt Hannah was a portrait painter, and Uncle Richard, Doctor Hardey's brother, was a photographer. Between them, they had a lively group of friends. The house was constantly filled with witty conversation and serious discussions about far-off places. Hudson enjoyed it all.

Everything was working out perfectly, or was it? Even though Hudson tried to push the thought to the back of his mind, one aspect of living with his aunt and uncle bothered him. A year earlier, Hudson had become convinced that the Bible instructed Christians to set aside one tenth of their income and give it to God's work, a practice the Bible calls tithing. So Hudson had begun giving one tenth of his income. Sometimes this had meant making sacrifices, but they were usually small, and he had always managed to get by. Now, though, he was beginning to think that his boarding allowance should also be included as part of his income and should be tithed. But there was one problem with doing this: If he gave one tenth of his boarding allowance to God's work, he would not have enough money left to live on.

A struggle raged within Hudson over the matter. Hadn't God provided him with a wonderful home to live in? Surely God didn't mean for him to tell his aunt and uncle they charged too much and he would have to leave and live somewhere else? In fact, the amount he paid his aunt and uncle was more than fair, especially when he took into account Aunt Hannah's wonderful cooking and the large size of his bedroom. How ungrateful he would seem if he left. And where would he go, anyway? The pressure from all these nagging questions built up within him, making it difficult to pray.

Finally, after wrestling with the matter for many weeks, Hudson made a decision. He decided that God did want him to tithe his boarding allowance, so he would have to find a cheaper place to live. He did some calculations to find out just how much rent he could afford to pay for a room after he'd paid his tithe.

Hudson found his options had narrowed right down to renting a room in Drainside, a not so glamorous place with a not so glamorous name. Sometimes we can read a place name, Station Street or Church Lane, for instance, and wonder how it got its name, since it has no station or church on it, at least not any longer. But this was not the case with Drainside. In Drainside, there was a real drain, and it was well used. People on both sides of the drain used it as their toilet, garbage disposal, and place to throw old furniture and broken household items. On hot days, the smell that rose from the drain was almost unbearable!

Now the drain happened to run right alongside the cottage of a Mrs. Finch, who had her front room for rent. Mrs. Finch was a Christian woman, raising several children on her own while her husband was at sea. Her husband sent her money when he could, but it was never quite enough, so she rented out her front room to help make ends meet. And it was to

Mrs. Finch's front room that Hudson moved. The room was simply furnished with a bed, table and chair, and a fireplace. No meals were provided, yet as Hudson arranged his books on the window sill, he was sure it was God's direction for him. Since there would be little socializing in the Finch cottage, he felt he would be able to spend more hours praying, studying for medical exams, and writing letters to Amelia and his parents and, of course, to Marianne, whom he still deeply loved.

Despite the change in living quarters, life felt good to Hudson. He could feel God drawing him closer to China and his destiny.

Each morning and evening, Hudson read his Bible. He read the great stories of faith contained in its pages, about David and Goliath, Daniel in the lion's den, and the disciples' healing the sick. As he read these stories, he was convinced that the Congregational minister back home in Barnsley had not been right. God was as much alive and active in 1852 as he had been in Bible days. *But*, Hudson wondered, *how does a person really learn to trust God and hear his voice in 1852, as those in the Bible did?* He knew he needed to learn to trust God in a new way and see Him answer his prayers before he ever dared to go to China.

Chapter 5

Waiting for Payday

Dr. Hardey paid Hudson his wages and boarding allowance every four months. Now, four months is a long time between paydays, and sometimes Hudson would run low on money, but he never ran completely out before the next payday arrived. It was a cold February day, two weeks before his next payday, and one of those times when Hudson was running low on money. Still, with some careful planning he knew he could make it through until Dr. Hardey paid him again. Payday was on Dr. Hardey's mind, too. As he left that evening, he said, "Hudson, you know how forgetful I am sometimes! Don't let me forget to pay you your wages when they are due."

Hudson was not against reminding people of things, but when Dr. Hardey said this, a strange thought came into his mind. Could this be one of the faith tests he'd been wanting? Was God asking him to stretch his faith? Instead of reminding Dr. Hardey when it was payday, did God want Hudson to trust Him to supply the money he needed? After spending some time praying about it, Hudson finally decided that indeed God was asking him to stretch his faith and trust Him for his needs. So he made an agreement with God: He would not ask Dr. Hardey for his money; he would trust God to supply his needs, no matter what happened.

Three weeks passed, and Hudson was feeling discouraged. Nothing had happened. He had asked God a hundred times a day to remind Dr. Hardey about his wages. Why wasn't God doing something? It was Saturday night, his rent was due in the morning, and Dr. Hardey was already a week late with his wages. The only money he had left was a single half-crown coin, and that was not enough to pay the rent. When was God going to act? And what would Mrs. Finch say if he couldn't pay the rent? Had he been foolish in promising God that he wouldn't ask for his wages? After all, Dr. Hardey owed him the money and would be more than pleased to pay it.

On Sunday morning, Hudson awoke feeling a little more full of faith. It was the Lord's day, and he felt sure this was the day he would get his money. He divided the remainder of his oatmeal in half and ate one portion for breakfast. He put the other half aside for dinner. He walked to church, watching the ground just in case someone had dropped some money that God intended for him to pick up. There was none, so he waited around a little longer after church, hoping that perhaps someone would slip some money into his pocket, but no one did. So, feeling a little discouraged again, he headed for Drainside and his room in Mrs. Finch's cottage. He had wanted to stretch his faith and trust God, but somehow things weren't working out like he'd planned.

To get to Drainside from church, Hudson had to walk through the roughest neighborhood in Hull. It was filled with Irish immigrants who found their new lives in England to be as dreary and poverty-filled as the ones they had left behind in Ireland. Yet despite its reputation for being unsafe and an area where policemen would travel only in groups of six or more, Hudson felt no fear. Most people recognized him as the young man who assisted Dr. Hardey. People here respected Dr. Hardey; they would never lay a hand on his assistant.

Hudson had walked about halfway through the area when a man he did not recognize came running up to him. The man grabbed Hudson by the arm and pulled him into an alley. "It's my wife. She's dying, I know she's dying," the man pleaded in a thick Irish accent. Hudson nodded. The man must have seen him with Dr. Hardey. The man went on, "I know you are a man of God, please come and pray for her." Hudson was surprised. The man seemed to want prayer more than medicine for his wife.

Hudson followed the man quickly, picking his way around heaps of garbage. Babies wailed from the three-storied buildings that loomed on either side of the alley. People sitting around outside nudged each other, and children peered around corners, curious as to which house the stranger was going to. It was not often such a well-dressed man ventured into their territory.

As he followed along, Hudson put his hand into his pocket and felt his last half-crown coin. *If only it were three smaller coins, I would gladly give the man a third of what I have,* Hudson thought to himself. Stepping around a pile of rotting vegetable peelings and corncobs, he stopped and looked up to where the man was pointing. "Up there," he said. "My missus is up there."

Hudson made his way up the iron staircase. Ragged clothes were hung to dry on the railing all the way up. At the top of the stairs, Hudson took a deep breath before opening the door. The smell in the room was almost unbearable. On a pile of rags in one corner lay a woman. Five hollow-cheeked children gathered around and stared blankly at her. A tiny baby lay still beside the woman's limp, pale body. Hudson had enough medical experience to know death was close at hand. The woman had probably bled during childbirth. Some superstitious old woman calling herself a midwife, with no idea of how to stop the bleeding, had probably been present for the birth. Instead of calling a doctor, she had left the woman to bleed, and now it was too late. Hudson had seen too many cases like this in his time with Dr. Hardey. And it was usually a double tragedy. Without a mother to feed it, the baby would die, too. And then there were the other five children. What would happen to them without a mother?

"Pray. Please pray," the woman's husband begged, entering the room behind Hudson.

Hudson thought again of the half crown in his pocket. *If only I had stopped at the bakery yesterday, I would have a one-shilling coin now that I could give to this man.* He cleared away an old newspaper to make room to kneel beside the woman.

The room was silent. The children stared at Hudson. The woman's husband closed his eyes and bowed his head. His wife stirred and again lost consciousness. Hudson felt he should say something comforting before he prayed. He cleared his throat. "Each of us needs to pray in our heart, trusting that God will answer our prayers. God is our Father, and He asks us to trust in Him, even when we cannot see with our natural eyes how things will get better. God asks us to use the eyes of our faith. He says He will never leave us or forsake us."

As he spoke, it was as if the room became a huge echo chamber. Everything he thought he was saying to this poor man and his family seemed to echo back at him five times louder. God was his Father, too. He had said He would never leave or forsake Hudson Taylor. So why didn't Hudson want to give away the whole half crown in his pocket? Wasn't it odd to be prepared to trust God to provide for him if there was still some money left in his pocket, but not if he gave it all away and his pocket was empty? Yes, he was prepared to share with these poor people, but surely God didn't intend for them to have all his money while he had none!

With all these questions running around inside his head, Hudson became too confused to continue talking. So he began to pray. Praying, he decided, would be easier than talking. He began reciting the Lord's prayer, figuring that the man and his children would be familiar with it and could pray along. "Our Father," he began. *See*, a voice prodded him inside his head, *God is our Father, as much their Father as He is yours. He is a Father who wants to provide for you and for them. Do you really believe that?*

Hudson stumbled as he recited the Lord's prayer. "Hallowed be thy name. Thy kingdom come..." But the prodding voice inside his head would not stop. *You're asking them to believe they're My children, but do you believe you are Mine? Do you believe I will look after you?"*

While the words of the Lord's prayer fell automatically from Hudson's lips, inside, his heart was in chaos. Finally he managed to finish the prayer and stood up. The man looked at his wife and baby and then at Hudson. "You can see what a terrible state we are in," he said. "If you can help us, for God's sake do."

Two Bible verses flashed through Hudson's mind: "Give to him that asks of you" and "In the word of a king there is power." Hudson knew what he had to do. He slid his hand into his pocket and pulled out the half crown. He handed the coin to the man, explaining as he did so that it was all the money he had in the world, but God was his Father and He provided for all of His children. As the man took the coin, peace and joy flooded into Hudson. Something deep inside had changed. Trusting God was no longer just a good idea; it was a new reality in his heart.

Hudson sang hymns to himself all the way back to Drainside. His heart felt as light as his pocket. When he arrived home, he ate the last of his oatmeal, without a thought as to where his next meal would come from.

Early the next morning, he heard the postman knock at the front door. He didn't pay much attention, since most of his mail arrived toward the end of the week. A moment later, though, there was a knock on *his* door. He opened it, and Mrs. Finch, wiping her wet hands on her apron, handed him a letter. *How curious that a letter should arrive on Monday,* he thought. He wondered who it could be from and studied the handwriting on the envelope. He did not recognize the writing. Then he looked at the postmark to see where it had been sent from, but it was smudged and unreadable. Finally, he opened the letter, and out dropped a pair of finely made men's gloves. He turned them over, hoping to find a note telling him who they were from, but there was no note. Then something small dropped from the envelope and fell to the floor. Hudson picked it up, amazed at what it was: a half-sovereign coin worth ten shillings, four times more than the half crown he had given away the night before. He immediately offered a prayer of thanks to God for meeting his needs.

In 1851, a half sovereign could last a person quite a while, particularly someone as frugal as Hudson Taylor. But after two weeks, he found himself in much the same position as before, with only a half-crown coin left in his pocket. Again he began pleading with God to remind Dr. Hardey that his wages were now long overdue. Of course, he knew he could have the money anytime he asked for it, and an apology from Dr. Hardey for being so late with it. But he'd made a promise that he would trust God to remind the doctor, and if he stepped in and took matters into his own hands, he felt he would be demonstrating a lack of faith. And if he couldn't trust God in this small thing, he wouldn't be able to trust God in all the adventures that would certainly await him in China.

So Hudson prayed and waited. Wednesday came and went, then Thursday and Friday. By Saturday he did not have a penny, and his rent was due, not to mention the fact that he had nothing left to eat. That evening as he boiled a pan of medicine and finished up his duties for the day, Dr. Hardey sat down to chat. He often had chats like this with Hudson. As they talked together, the doctor looked over at Hudson with a questioning look. "By the way," he asked, "isn't your salary due again?"

Hudson concentrated hard on the pan of boiling medicine he was stirring, trying not to let the doctor see how excited he was. Finally he answered as casually as he could, "I think it was due a while ago."

"I wish you had reminded me," said Dr. Hardey. "I'm sorry. I got busy and totally forgot your wages. I would pay you right now, but I sent all the money to the bank this afternoon. I won't have any cash until Monday."

Hudson quickly turned back to the pan, this time trying to hide his disappointment. One moment he was sure God had answered his prayers, the next his hopes were dashed into a thousand pieces.

Thankfully, Dr. Hardey left the surgery for home soon after. Hudson didn't want him to see how disappointed he was. As soon as the doctor had left, Hudson lifted the pan of medicine off the burner and knelt down beside a chair to pray. His prayer started out as a prayer of panic, but after a while, he began to feel peace within. God had told him to trust and be patient, and that was what he would do.

By the time Hudson had finished all his duties, it was 10 P.M. He put on his overcoat and readied himself to brave the cold walk back to his room at Drainside. At least he wouldn't have to face Mrs. Finch and tell her he had no money to pay the rent. Thankfully Mrs. Finch always went to bed early on Saturday evenings.

Hudson was just reaching to turn off the office's gaslight when he heard someone laughing outside. Then Dr. Hardey burst through the door. "What a funny thing just happened to me," he said. "I was getting ready for bed when I heard a knock at the door. It was Mr. Pritchard, one of my wealthiest patients. He was standing on my doorstep wanting to pay his bill." Dr. Hardey shook his head as he went on. "What would possess a man to pay a bill at 10 o'clock on a Saturday night? And he didn't pay by check as he usually does, he gave me cash instead."

The doctor reached for the ledger book and entered the payment in it. He was still chuckling to himself about his late-night visitor as he walked towards the door. As he turned to close it behind him, he remembered something. "By the way, Taylor, you might as well take these notes. I'll give you the balance of your wages next week. And one other thing. I was seeing to a patient on the other side of town the other day when an Irishman came up to me and said to tell you thank you for your prayer; his wife has made a full recovery." With that he handed Hudson a wad of bank notes and then walked out, shutting the door behind him.

Hudson stood in stunned silence as goosebumps ran up his arms. It was ten minutes after ten, and here he was holding enough money to pay Mrs. Finch his rent on time and buy food for breakfast. And not only that, the woman he'd prayed for had made a full recovery. He was so certain she was going to die. But God had answered his prayer. Now he knew, no matter what, he had the faith to trust God in all that lay ahead of him in China.

Chapter 6

A Dead Man in London

Taylor, how would you like to be my apprentice?" Dr. Hardey asked after Hudson had been his assistant in Hull for about a year.

Hudson's mouth dropped open. He stopped mixing the medicine he was preparing and turned to the doctor with a questioning look.

"You heard me right," said the doctor. "I want you to become my apprentice. It will be five years of hard study for you, but I know you can do it. You have what it takes to be a good doctor."

"Thank you, sir," replied Hudson, stunned by the offer. "It's a great honor to be asked. I'll have to pray about it before I give you an answer."

Dr. Hardey nodded; he had expected no less. He knew Hudson prayed about everything.

It was such a tempting offer. Hudson liked the idea of being a real doctor rather than a doctor's assistant. But the more he thought and prayed about it, the more convinced he became that he should reject the offer. While he could see the advantage of being a qualified doctor, he also recognized that inside of him was a burning desire to be in China as soon as he could. Yes, he needed more medical training before he left, but he thought he could get that training faster by going to London. So he decided to turn down Dr. Hardey's offer and resign as his assistant.

He also talked to his parents about his decision. He knew that the offer was a wonderful opportunity, so it was arranged that Mr. Taylor would release Hudson's cousin, John, from work in the pharmacy so he could come to Hull and be Dr. Hardey's new assistant.

A week after announcing his resignation as Dr. Hardey's assistant, things began to fall into place for Hudson. Uncle Benjamin, whom Hudson and Amelia had stayed with on their first trip to London, offered to have Hudson stay with him for a week or two. And the Chinese Evangelization Society agreed to pay Hudson's medical tuition at London Hospital. Hoping to get a doctor into Inland China as soon as possible, the society was more generous to Hudson than he could have imagined. It offered to provide his rent money as well. At the same time, Hudson's father also volunteered to support him while he was in London. Instead of having no financial aid, Hudson now had offers from two sources!

But which proposal should he accept? He didn't want to get too indebted to the Chinese Evangelization Society in case things did not work out in China. He also wasn't sure he wanted to get too tied to one organization in case God called him do things on his own. Accepting his father's aid, though, would also be difficult. His father was not doing well financially, and Hudson knew the offer represented a big sacrifice for the family. As he considered whose support to accept, he wrote to both his father and the Chinese Evangelization Society, letting each one know about the other's willingness to support him and promising to make a decision soon.

As he prayed about the decision before him, a strange thought crept into his mind. What if he turned them both down! What an ideal way to stretch his faith a little more. Could he rely on God, and not on his father or the Chinese Evangelization Society, to meet his needs? He would be in a new city where nobody knew him. What a perfect opportunity to trust God to supply his needs. Immediately, Hudson felt that this was what God wanted him to do. He picked up his pen and wrote another pair of letters, the first to his father and the other to the Chinese Evangelization Society, thanking them for their offer of support and telling them he would not be accepting it. As he wrote, he decided that they would both think he had accepted the other's offer. It was perfect. He would be free to rely on God alone to meet his needs without other people, especially his mother, worrying about how he was doing.

Two weeks later, in early September 1852, he stood at the bow of a coastal steamship headed for London. As the ship carefully made its way through the thick fog that blanketed the banks of the river Thames, he pulled his overcoat tight around him to keep out the cold, damp air. What lay ahead for him he did not know. *One thing is for sure,* he promised himself, *the next time I stand on board a ship, it will be headed for China.*

The boarding house where Uncle Benjamin lived was small but comfortable, and Hudson spent two enjoyable weeks with him. In another boarding house, just around the corner, his cousin Tom lived in a tiny third-floor attic room. Tom invited Hudson to move in and share the room with him. Hudson lugged his belongings up the three flights of stairs to Tom's room. He enrolled in a surgery course at London Hospital in Whitechapel, and once again his life quickly fell into a routine of work, study, prayer, and fellowship, not to mention the time he spent each day practicing writing Chinese pictographs.

Hudson had managed to save a little money during his time in Hull, and he was determined to make it go as far as possible. To do this, he experimented until he came up with a diet that cost very little and did not leave him feeling too hungry. On the walk home from London Hospital, he would stop at a bakery and buy a two-penny loaf of brown bread. He would have the baker cut the loaf in half. One half of the loaf was his dinner, and the other half would be his breakfast. Of course, he could have cut the loaf in half himself, but he asked the baker to do it because he thought his hunger might tempt him to cut too large a "half" for dinner, leaving too small a piece to satisfy his hunger at breakfast. On the way to the hospital in the morning, he would stop at a fruit stand and buy two apples for his lunch. When he was thirsty, he drank water. By eating only apples and bread and drinking water, Hudson was able to live on three pennies a day, plus what he paid his cousin for half the rent on the attic room.

To save himself even more money, Hudson walked everywhere he needed to go. He walked four miles to the hospital in Whitechapel and back each day. He walked to church on Sunday. He also walked a four-mile round trip to the shipping office once a month. He went to the shipping office as a favor for Mrs. Finch, his former landlady in Hull. Mrs. Finch's husband was a ship's officer for a shipping line that operated out of London. Half of his wages were kept at the office for Mrs. Finch to collect. Normally Mrs. Finch had the money sent up to her in Hull, but there was a charge for this service. So she had asked Hudson if he would go to the shipping office for her once a month to collect her husband's wages and send them to her. This way she would save having to pay the service charge. Mrs. Finch had been good to Hudson in Hull, and he knew she needed all the money she could get, so he was happy to do the favor for her.

Hudson had been in London about three months when he got a letter from Mrs. Finch saying she needed the money from her husband's wages right away because she was about to fall behind in her rent. Hudson was very busy with his studies right then and did not think he could spare the time to walk to the shipping office to collect the money. Without giving it much thought, he decided to send Mrs. Finch the last of his own money. He would go later in the week and collect her husband's wages and repay himself from that. This way they would both be happy: Mrs. Finch would quickly get the money she desperately needed, and Hudson would not have to give up half a day of study to get it for her.

There was just one problem with this solution, however. When Hudson finally went to the shipping office to get Mr. Finch's wages, he got some bad news. Mr. Finch, it seemed, had abandoned his ship and headed for a gold rush. Since Mr. Finch was no longer on board ship, there were no wages to collect. Hudson was stunned. He explained to the clerk in the shipping office how he had just sent Mrs. Finch the last of his money and now had no way of being repaid. The clerk was sympathetic; he even apologized for Mr. Finch's behavior. But he pointed out to Hudson that men deserted their ships and their families every day, and there was nothing that could be done about it.

It took a few moments for the seriousness of the situation to settle in on Hudson. He had only a few pennies left. And not only was he not going to be repaid for the money he'd already sent to Mrs. Finch, she was not going to get any more money from her husband to pay her rent and take care of the children.

Hudson left the office and began the walk home. It would have been normal to be depressed by such news, but as he walked on, he found himself getting happier and happier. When he had arrived in London, his intention was to trust God to provide all his needs, but he'd always had the money he'd saved in Hull to get by on. Hudson's money would have eventually run out, leaving him no other option but to rely on God. Mr. Finch and his gold-digging ambitions had only brought that day about sooner. By the time Hudson climbed the stairs to his attic room, he was excited about what would happen next. How would God meet his needs?

That night, Hudson continued with his studies. He had to stop for a few minutes to make himself a new notebook. It was cheaper for him to make his own notebook than buy a ready-made one from the store. To make the notebook, he took a stack of blank paper and hand sewed it together. Just as he was finishing the last stitch, the needle jerked through the paper and pricked him in the finger. There was no blood, and a minute later Hudson had forgotten all about the prick. That was, until the next day.

It was noon and Hudson was sitting in a lecture when he began to feel sick. The room started to swirl around him, and he could no longer concentrate on what the lecturer was saying. Hudson stumbled outside into the fresh air and had a drink of water. He felt revived, so he made his way back to the lecture hall. He thought he must have overexerted himself the day before walking to the shipping office and staying up late to study. Back in the lecture hall he began to feel weaker and weaker, until he was too weak to even hold the pencil he was taking notes with. Obviously, he hadn't exhausted his fingers walking to the shipping office or sitting up late to study! Something else was wrong.

After the lecture, he dragged himself back into the surgery, where earlier that day he and some of the other students had been dissecting the body of a man who had died of malignant fever. He knew he should help the other students clean up, but all he could do was slump into the nearest chair.

"I don't know what's come over me," he said to the surgeon in charge of the dissection. Then he described his symptoms.

The surgeon went pale. He cleared his throat several times before finally speaking. "What has happened to you is clear enough. You must have cut yourself while dissecting the body and infected yourself with the malignant fever."

Hudson shook his head. "That's not possible. I

would know if I cut myself with the scalpel, and I'm sure I didn't. Here, look at my hands."

As Hudson raised his hands for the surgeon to inspect, a thought crossed his mind. "It couldn't be a pinprick I gave myself while sewing a book together last night, could it?"

The surgeon thought for a moment. "It doesn't take a large opening to let in an infection." He reached forward and put his hand on Hudson's shoulder. Then, lowering his voice and looking straight into Hudson's blue eyes, he said, "You must get a coach home as quickly as you can and get your affairs in order, for you are a dead man!"

Hudson couldn't believe what he'd just heard. It wasn't that he doubted the surgeon's diagnosis, or that he thought people survived malignant fever— they normally didn't. What Hudson couldn't believe was that he wouldn't make it to China after all. "I am not afraid to die," he said, looking straight at the surgeon. "In fact, I look forward to meeting my Maker. But unless I am very much mistaken, I cannot die because God has called me to China, and I have not yet been there. I may get very sick, but I doubt that I will die."

The surgeon was surprised. "This is a fine time for you to argue with me as to why you shouldn't die," he said. "Accept the inevitable. Get home as quickly as you can, or you will not make it home at all."

Hudson did go home. At first he tried to walk, but he was too weak, so he used his last penny to catch a horse-drawn omnibus. As it rattled along the uneven cobblestone streets, Hudson had to concentrate hard to stay awake. If he fell asleep, he might go right past his stop. Eventually the omnibus came to a stop near the boarding house, where Hudson practically fell out of the vehicle.

The maid met him at the door, and he asked her to get him some hot water. He began climbing up the three flights of stairs that led to his room. He was crawling by the time he got to the top. He had just enough strength left to reach up and turn the doorknob. He crawled into the room, and the maid soon followed with a bowl of hot water which she set down on the floor beside him. Hudson put his hand in the basin of water. After soaking it a minute or two, he took a scalpel from his jacket pocket, clamped his teeth together, and, before he could change his mind, sliced the scalpel into the finger he'd pricked the night before. Searing pain shot up his arm. He dropped the scalpel and began squeezing the wound he'd made on his finger as hard as he could, hoping to squeeze out all of the malignant fever. Blood spurted out, and as it did so, Hudson's grip loosened, and he slumped backwards and faded from consciousness.

The next thing Hudson knew, he was being dragged into his bed and shaken awake by Uncle Benjamin. As Hudson regained consciousness, Uncle Benjamin told him he'd sent for his own doctor, and soon one of the best doctors in London was standing beside the bed. He examined Hudson from head to toe and confirmed the malignant fever diagnosis. The doctor had one word of hope to offer Hudson. "If you have been living moderately, and not drinking beer late into the night, you might pull through. If you have been drinking and partying, I don't see any hope for you," he said.

Hudson would have laughed if his ribs didn't ache so badly. "If it's a matter of sober living, then I have more chance of making it than just about anyone I know," he whispered to the doctor with a smile.

"It's going to be a hard battle. You will be in and out of consciousness a lot, and if you do recover, it will be months before you are back to your old self. You need to keep your strength up, drink port wine, and eat as many beef chops as you can," the doctor advised him.

Hudson tried to concentrate, but the doctor's words faded away as he lost consciousness. He spent several days drifting in and out of consciousness. Uncle Benjamin and Tom took turns looking after him and feeding him the wine and chops the doctor had ordered. Each day the doctor came by to give him quinine to help fight the fever. Hudson was in this zone between life and death for many days. Finally he seemed to turn a corner and begin to get better. Before long he was sitting up in bed, receiving visitors. On one visit, a fellow student told him how two students from a neighboring hospital had both accidentally cut themselves during the dissection of a dead body. Both of them had died. Hudson shuddered. God had truly spared his life so he could go to China.

It was only a few days later that Hudson felt well enough to walk downstairs. Tom helped him, and slowly they made their way down to the parlor. Hudson slumped onto the sofa, exhausted from the effort. But how good it felt to be out of his bedroom. When the doctor arrived to check in on him, he was amazed to find Hudson downstairs in the parlor. The doctor worried about how he would make it up the stairs again. After checking his patient over and asking a few questions, he suggested that Hudson go to the country as soon as his health would allow it. The fresh air and wholesome food would do him good.

Hudson thought about the doctor's advice for a while. It would be good to go home. For once, the thought of his mother fussing over him seemed wonderful. But there was the matter of money. He didn't have enough for the train trip back to Barnsley. And if he did get any money, it would surely have to go towards paying the doctor for all his care.

Alone in the parlor, Hudson began to pray about his situation. And as he prayed, he kept feeling that he should go back to the shipping office. Part of him thought this was a crazy idea, like clutching at straws. But another part of him felt that God was directing him to go there. After about an hour, he came to the firm conclusion that God was indeed leading him to go. But when should he go? That was the question. He had been in bed in a weakened state for days. It had taken all his energy to get down the stairs to the parlor, and like the doctor, he too was having doubts about his ability to climb back up them. It would obviously be some time before he could make it to the shipping office. Or would it? There was that little voice in his head again, reminding him that God says all things are possible to those who believe. Hudson believed, so he told God he was willing to make the two-mile walk to the office if God would give him the strength to do it. When he had finished telling this to God, as sick as he still was, a tremendous peace came over him. He asked the maid to fetch his hat and walking stick from upstairs. With a surprised look on her face, she headed off upstairs. When she came back, Hudson was standing at the front door, ready to walk to the shipping office.

Hudson set himself a slow pace. He walked past two shop fronts and stopped for breath at the third. When he came to a hill, he allowed himself to stop at every shop front. In this way, he slowly wound his way through the streets of London. As he walked and stumbled along, he wondered what God's purpose for this trip would turn out to be. Finally, he sat down heavily on the front steps of the building that housed the shipping office. Businessmen stepped around him as he sat and panted and waited for the strength to climb the stairs to the second-floor office.

Eventually Hudson lumbered up the stairs and entered the shipping office. A look of relief spread across the face of the clerk as he entered. "I'm so glad to see you again, sir," he said, as Hudson flopped into the nearest chair. "I didn't know how to contact you. I have some good news. There were two Mr. Finches on the same boat, and it was the other one, not your Mr. Finch, that ran off to the gold fields. It was all a mix-up and I am very sorry. Here is the money we owe you." He handed Hudson an envelope filled with money.

The clerk went on to ask Hudson about his health, then insisted that he stay and share lunch before heading back home, on an omnibus, of course.

The next day Hudson went to pay the doctor, but since Hudson was in the same profession, the doctor refused payment. Hudson, though, insisted on at least paying for the quinine. The doctor accepted the money, then told Hudson he wasn't yet strong enough to be out walking around. Hudson told him the story of going to the shipping office the day before. "Impossible!" interrupted the doctor. "Why, I left you lying in the parlor more like a ghost than a man." Hudson had to assure the doctor over and over that with God's help, he really had walked all that way. By the time he left the surgery, the doctor was nearly in tears. "I would give all the world to have a faith like yours," he said, shaking Hudson's hand.

"You can, it's free for the asking," Hudson replied as he turned to leave.

There was just enough money left after paying the doctor for Hudson to buy a train ticket to

Barnsley and some good food to eat on the way, and to hire a wagon to take him right to his parents' home when he got there.

God, it seemed, had everything under control after all.

Chapter 7

"Were You to Remain in England"

Back in Barnsley, Hudson made a quick recovery. The house was warm, the food wholesome, and his mother fussed over him constantly, especially after she found out about his eating habits in London. Amelia and Marianne were also frequent visitors to the house, and their laughter and conversation cheered him. On one of these visits, Hudson finally plucked up the courage to ask Marianne to marry him. He was excited when she agreed and her father gave his permission. Marianne would be his companion in China after all!

After several weeks at home, Hudson received news that his cousin Tom, in London, was sick with rheumatic fever. Since Tom had cared for him when he was sick with malignant fever, Hudson thought it was time to return the favor, so he traveled back to London.

As he sat through the nights caring for Tom, he continually prayed for God to provide a way for him to get to China sooner rather than later.

Unknown to Hudson, as he stood watch beside Tom's bed, things were happening in China. Since 1644, China had been ruled by an emperor and governing officials who were Manchu people from northeastern China. The Manchu emperor and his government were known as the Qing dynasty. But even though outsiders thought everyone in China was the same, the Chinese people regarded the Manchus as alien outsiders. Of course, this didn't really worry the Qing dynasty. They had been in power for a long, long time, and they had more than enough troops to keep things that way. Or so they thought. In central China, a long way from Peking, the Qing dynasty's capital, a rebellion had begun, and it was getting bigger with each passing day. The rebellion was known as the Taiping Rebellion, and those fighting in the rebellion were fighting to overthrow the Qing dynasty. Soon the Taipings had control of much of central China, including the old capital of Nanking. But more important for Europeans than how much territory the Taipings controlled was what their leaders thought about white people. While they wanted the English to stop importing opium into China, the Taipings did not believe that white people were "barbarians," as many Chinese people did. Instead they believed that all men were brothers and that, rather than being kept out of the interior of China, white people should be allowed to go where they wished and meet with whomever they wanted.

News of the rebellion slowly drifted back to England, and Hudson first read about it in *The Gleaner,* the newsletter of the Chinese Evangelization Society. He was excited by what he read, but he was also very busy. While taking care of Tom, he had once again run out of money. This time, though, he felt God had a different plan to meet his needs than before. And sure enough, as Hudson prayed about the situation, Dr. Brown from the Bishopsgate area of London offered him a job as his assistant. Not only that, Dr. Brown offered to adjust the hours Hudson worked so that he could continue his medical studies at London Hospital.

Hudson eagerly accepted the position, and since Tom was well enough, he moved in with Dr. Brown and his wife. Soon Hudson's days were full. After attending classes at the hospital from eight in the morning until three in the afternoon, it was back to Bishopsgate, where he assisted Dr. Brown dispensing medicine, visiting patients, and keeping the doctor's accounts. When he had finished helping Dr. Brown in the evening, Hudson prayed, studied the Bible, pored over his medical books, and practiced writing Chinese pictographs late into the night. The days were long, but Mrs. Brown's wonderful cooking seemed to give Hudson the energy he needed to keep going.

Marianne made trips to London to visit Hudson, but with each trip, he couldn't help noticing that Marianne did not seem to share his enthusiasm. She always had a reason for why she could not stay longer. Finally, after several weeks, he confronted her about it, and she confessed that she did love him, but her mother was very ill, and her father had never really approved of their engagement. Hudson was shocked: Her father had personally given them permission to marry.

Immediately, he wrote to Mr. Vaughan to set things straight. Mr. Vaughan responded very straightforwardly, though not as Hudson wanted or expected. His letter read: "Were you to remain in England, nothing would give me more pleasure than to see you happily married to Marianne. But, though I do not forbid your connection, I feel I can never willingly give her up, or ever think of her leaving this country."

At first Hudson felt angry at Mr. Vaughan. *Why did he say yes to the marriage in the first place? Why didn't he say what he really felt in the beginning?* But the more he thought about it, the more he could sympathize with the way Mr. Vaughan felt. Over and over in his mind he played an imaginary conversation with Mr. Vaughan. The conversation went like this:

Mr. Vaughan: *"Where are you going to live once you are married?"*

Hudson: *"China."*

Mr. Vaughan: *"What part of China? After all, China is a very big country."*

Hudson: *"I don't know yet, God hasn't shown me. But I believe it will be somewhere in the interior, somewhere where foreigners have never been."*

Mr. Vaughan: *"What means of support will you have?"*

Hudson: *"The Chinese Evangelization Society might send me out, but I have not fully decided to take up their offer, nor are they financially stable. In short, we will go with nothing except what God supplies."*

Mr. Vaughan: *"How often will you bring Marianne home to visit her family?"*

Hudson: *"I can't promise you that you'll ever see her again."*

When Hudson thought about things this way, it was easy to see why Mr. Vaughan was not eager for them to marry. But he loved Marianne. He was convinced she would make a wonderful wife. Of course, he could always not go to China. Marianne was always telling him that he could help many people at home in England as a doctor. Yet as much as he loved Marianne, he loved God more, and God had called him to China, with or without a wife. There was nothing left to do but end the engagement.

Although he was depressed over the breakup with Marianne, he was excited by the stories of the Taiping Rebellion that continued to be reported in *The Gleaner.* There was great optimism among churches and missionary societies that this could be the break they were all looking for, the break that would once and for all let missionaries penetrate into Inland China. With his head full of the events taking place in China, Hudson sometimes found it hard to focus on his medical studies.

It was at this time a major thought occurred to him. Yes, he loved medicine and the idea of being a doctor, but medical knowledge was simply a tool. He was called to be an evangelist, and if his medical training helped him to evangelize more effectively, then well and good. But one thing was for sure, he knew he wasn't called to China to just start a hospital in one of the Treaty Ports. He was called to evangelize Inland China. And now the Taiping Rebellion seemed to be providing a wonderful opportunity to finally get where he knew he was called, deep into the very heart of China. So why should he continue on with his medical training when it was training him to be something he knew God hadn't called him to be? No, it was time for him to be on his way to China.

At the same time that Hudson was having these thoughts, the Chinese Evangelization Society decided that the present opportunity in China was too good to miss. They decided to send two missionaries there immediately. When the society found out that Hudson Taylor was available, they soon decided that he should be the first to go. The Chinese Evangelization Society would pay for his trip to China and would send him money each month to meet his living expenses. He would go first to Shanghai and wait there until opportunities opened up for him to move farther inland.

Hudson was delighted.

The Chinese Evangelization Society booked him passage to China on the *Dumfries*, a two-masted sailing ship leaving from Liverpool on September 19 headed for Shanghai. Hudson quickly set about gathering the supplies he needed to take with him. Finally, several days before the *Dumfries* was due to sail, he arrived in Liverpool, where his family was waiting for him. Mr. Pearse from the Chinese Evangelization Society also joined them, as did Aunt Hannah. They all spent several wonderful days together.

Finally, September 19, 1853, arrived. The crew were just stowing the last of the cargo when Hudson arrived at the dock. Hudson went aboard, and the steward showed him to his cabin in the stern of the ship. The cabin had been freshly painted in honor of the only passenger of the trip. His family, Mr. Pearse, and a local minister all accompanied him to his cabin, where they prayed and read Psalms together. Finally, they had to leave the ship, as it was about to set sail. Hudson hugged his mother one last time, and when she was safely back on the dock, the mooring ropes were let go and the *Dumfries* slid away from the dock out into the Mersey River. Captain Morris gave the order to hoist the sails, and as the wind caught them, the ship began the three-mile trip down the Mersey to the Irish Sea. Hudson waved as hard as he could at his family on the dock, and as they began to fade from sight, he climbed into the rigging in hopes of getting one last look. He was twenty-one years old and on his way to China at last.

Four days out from Liverpool, the *Dumfries* ran into the fierce storm that nearly wrecked it and its crew on the rocks of the Welsh coast. It took Captain Morris and his crew nearly two weeks to repair all the damage done to the ship by the storm. Some of the crew had been injured in the storm, and Hudson was able to tend to their wounds. Finally, with all the damage repaired, the ship was able to get back under full sail as she headed down the west coast of Africa.

After the excitement of the storm in the Irish Sea had passed, the voyage soon become monotonous. At Christmastime, three months after leaving Liverpool, the ship reached the southernmost point on her voyage: the Cape of Good Hope. The *Dumfries'* log showed that the ship had traveled 14,500 miles so far, but there was still a long way to go before she reached China.

By early January 1854, the *Dumfries* had begun the long haul across the Indian Ocean. She passed 120 miles off the northwestern tip of Australia and headed out among the tropical islands of the western Pacific Ocean for the last, slow leg of her voyage to Shanghai. Occasionally, she came close enough to an island for the inhabitants to paddle out to the ship to offer coconuts and shells in exchange for knives or blankets.

Days and nights in the tropics settled into a pattern. During the day the sea was calm and there was no wind, so the sailors would play cards, carve scrimshaw, and entertain each other with stories of what they would do when they got ashore. Occasionally, one of them would slip away from the group and stop by Hudson's cabin. His door was always open, and he had many interesting discussions with crew members about aspects of the Sunday services he held on deck. At sunset the wind usually began to blow. If they were lucky, it would continue blowing until dawn. Some nights, though, the wind didn't come at all. On those nights, the *Dumfries* covered less than seven miles. Captain Morris faithfully entered the distance covered each day into the ship's log.

If their journey had begun with near disaster because of the overactivity of the wind and waves, it nearly ended in disaster for the exact opposite reason.

It was Sunday, and Hudson was holding his regular service on the aft deck of the *Dumfries*. Many crewmen sat around on barrels and coils of rope, listening as he preached, but Captain Morris didn't seem to be paying attention to the service. This was unusual. The captain was a Methodist and thoroughly enjoyed having a young missionary aboard his ship. After the final hymn was sung, the captain walked to the side of the ship and peered worriedly into the water. Hudson joined him and asked what he was looking for. The answer was not comforting. They were becalmed and headed for disaster. The current was stronger than usual, about four knots, and it was carrying them towards a sunken reef. With no wind expected until nightfall, Captain

Morris feared it would be too late, and the *Dumfries* would hit the reef and sink before then. This information sent shudders up Hudson's spine. He had seen many sharks around the ship in the past few days, and he did not like the thought of having to swim for his life.

Becalmed is one word that strikes fear into the hearts of men on sailing ships. A storm, even a hurricane, can often be outrun, but a becalmed ship goes wherever the current takes it, and there is nothing that can be done about it. In the Irish Sea, the *Dumfries* had nearly been lost because of too much wind. Now, it seemed, she would be lost because of too little wind. It was a desperate situation. And even though Captain Morris knew that nothing could be done about the wind, his crew begged him to let them try something. So he allowed them to put to sea in the longboats. They connected heavy ropes from the *Dumfries* to the longboats and then strained at the oars, trying to row the ship against the current. But she would not be swayed and continued to drift.

Silently, the crew climbed the rope net back on board the *Dumfries*. Their best efforts had done no good. It was hopeless. By the time the evening breeze came, it would be far too late for the ship and her crew.

How strange to meet death on such a calm and beautiful day, Hudson thought as he peered over the side of the *Dumfries*. Then Captain Morris broke into his thoughts. "We've done everything we can," he said. "We can only wait and see what happens next."

The captain's words echoed in Hudson's head. *We've done everything we can...*but had they?

An idea came to him. Enthusiastically, he turned to Captain Morris and said, "There is one thing we have not done yet."

"And what is that?" asked the captain, surprised that Hudson would think he knew something about rescuing becalmed ships.

"Four of us on board are Christians. Let's each go to his own cabin and agree together to pray and ask God to give us wind right away. He can just as easily send it now as at sunset."

Captain Morris agreed, since no one but God could help them now. He hurried off to his cabin while Hudson located the ship's Swedish carpenter and the steward, the other two Christians aboard.

In his cabin, Hudson prayed hard for a few minutes and then felt as though some burden had been lifted from him. He was confident that God had heard their prayers and would answer them. Getting up off his knees, he strode back up on deck. The first officer was standing, smoking a pipe on the foredeck.

"Hurry, let the mainsail down all the way," Hudson told him.

The first officer sneered at him, "What would be the point of that?"

"The Christians on board have been praying for wind, and it will come any moment now. I suggest you get ready for it."

The first officer laughed heartily. A young missionary was telling him how to run a ship. There would be no wind until sunset, and to make his point, he turned toward the sail. Did it flutter a little? Perhaps. But a flutter would do them no good.

As the first officer stood there, a much stronger gust of wind swept across the ship. This time he wasted no time. "All hands on deck," he yelled, as he grabbed hold of one of the halyards. The crew came running, and not far behind them was Captain Morris, who had heard all the commotion from his cabin. It was a wonderful, strong breeze that blew. Within minutes the *Dumfries* was ploughing through the Pacific Ocean at seven knots. Each minute that passed took them farther away from the dangerous reef and closer to Shanghai.

Chapter 8

China at Last

Hudson looked over the side of the *Dumfries* and saw Chinese soil. Not dry land, but soil—tons of it, mixed with water and tumbling out of the Yangtze River. Captain Morris had told him they were at anchor in the river mouth. Hudson would not have otherwise known, because a cold damp fog pressed so tightly around the ship that it was impossible to make out land on either side. They had dropped anchor to wait for the harbor pilot to arrive and guide them first to Woo-sung, then fifteen miles on up the Hwang-poo River to the docks of Shanghai.

Like the rest of the crew, after five and a half months at sea, Hudson was eager to hear any news the pilot might have of England and the situation with the Taiping Rebellion. But there wasn't much to do while he waited for the harbor pilot to arrive. So he packed and repacked his trunk several times, then went up and paced the well-worn decks of the *Dumfries*. He peered into the foggy whiteness, hoping to catch a glimpse of land. It was so frustrating. He had been preparing for five years to come to China, and now that he was here he couldn't even see it.

Finally, he gave up and went below to write one last journal entry from the *Dumfries*. "What peculiar feelings arise at the prospect of soon landing in an unknown country, in the midst of strangers—a country now to be my home and sphere of labor," he wrote.

He put down his pen and tried to imagine what he would do when he finally reached Shanghai. He glanced at the three neatly stacked letters lying on top of his Bible. Thank goodness he had them; they were his link to a new life in China. The top two were letters of introduction from good friends in England to missionaries they knew in Shanghai. On the strength of their friendship and the letters, Hudson knew either missionary would be happy to advise him as he began his new life. The third letter was from a casual acquaintance in London to the prestigious Dr. Walter Medhurst of the London Missionary Society. Dr. Medhurst had written the book on China that Hudson had borrowed from the Congregational minister in Barnsley—the book that had influenced him to pursue medical training.

He tried to keep writing in his journal, but his mind kept wandering. *What was China like now? Had the Taiping Rebellion finally been victorious over the Qing dynasty?* There had been so many wonderful reports about what was happening before he left England. Had inland China opened up during the time he'd been at sea? He could hardly wait to find out.

As he picked up his pen to write some more, he heard the first mate yell, "Boat to starboard, all hands on deck."

Hudson quickly blotted the ink dry and shut his journal. Excitement pulsed through his veins as he raced up on deck. He followed the gaze of the crew. Coming towards them like a gliding bird was a Chinese junk. Hudson stood and stared. He felt like he was living inside a picture book. He strained to see the Chinese sailors, and as the junk moved closer they became distinct individuals. They were all wearing dark blue pajama-like suits. As they moved, he could see their pigtails, or queues, as the Chinese called them, swaying behind them. A feeling of thankfulness came over Hudson. The years of preparing and waiting were over; the voyage was behind him. Come what may, God had brought him faithfully to China, and for the first time, he was seeing Chinese people face to face.

The *Dumfries'* crew scrambled to catch the bowline as it was thrown from the junk. Soon the ship was tied up safely alongside, and a single Englishman emerged from among the Chinese sailors. He climbed the rope ladder that had been lowered over the side of the ship. When he finally stepped on deck, a cheer went up from the *Dumfries'* crew. Their pilot had arrived. They would soon be on their way up the river to Shanghai.

The junk soon faded into the fog as effortlessly as it had come. The crew waited anxiously while the pilot and Captain Morris spoke together in the captain's cabin. When they came out, the pilot informed them that instead of lifting, the fog was getting thicker. They would not be going anywhere today and probably not tomorrow either; it was just too dangerous to try to navigate the river in this kind of weather. Hudson was disappointed. But he soon entered into the spirit of things and, with the rest of the crew, began pumping the pilot for news of home.

The pilot told them Turkey and Russia were readying their armies to fight each other on the Crimean Peninsula. England and France had sent their Navies, and they were also sending troops to back up the Russians.

Had Queen Victoria sent the troops as a warning, or did she mean for them to fight? the crew wanted to know. *How many English soldiers had been sent? Would more be going? Had the French sent as many soldiers as the English?* Behind the questions lay the anxiety of twenty-three men, wondering whether their brothers and sons might be already fighting in the Crimea.

The pilot told them all he knew of the situation in the Crimea and then went on to tell them some local news. The crew were not nearly as interested in it, but Hudson was. China was his new home, and he wanted to know what was going on. The pilot had news of the Taiping Rebellion. When Hudson had left England five-and-a-half months ago, it seemed the rebellion would open up the heart of China to foreigners. He hoped it had by now, because he intended to stay in Shanghai only a short time before heading inland to explore and evangelize. But the news the pilot was giving him was very different from the rosy picture that had been reported back in England. The Taiping Rebellion had turned very violent. In Shanghai, a group of Taiping rebels known as the "Red Turbans," named after the red turbans they wore, had seized control of the city. The city was now surrounded by thousands of Imperial troops who intended to take it back from the Red Turbans by force. A bloody civil war was raging.

Shanghai was divided into two parts, the old Chinese walled city, which the Red Turbans had actually seized, and the International Settlement, set up after the Opium War as a place for foreigners to live and trade. Unfortunately, the International Settlement was located outside the old city wall to the north and was caught right between the two opposing forces.

The two sides were busy firing cannons back and forth over the wall at each other. And, as so often happens in war, civilians were the main casualties. Hundreds of homes had been destroyed and thousands of people displaced.

As Hudson listened to the pilot speak, his heart sank. This was not at all what he'd expected. It was not how he had imagined things would be during the long months at sea. But there was even more bad news for Hudson. Because Shanghai was under siege, transporting even common things like rice and vegetables into the city was so dangerous that the prices of everything had skyrocketed. In the past month alone, prices had doubled, and the rate of increase didn't seem to be slowing. Rent, too, had gone up, that is, if you were lucky enough to find a place to rent. With so many buildings and homes destroyed, it was almost impossible to find a house or room for rent in the city. This was particularly bad news for Hudson, who had nothing but a few shillings left in his pocket with which to support himself until he got more money from the Chinese Evangelization Society. Still, he had come this far, and he felt sure God would not let him down now.

As dawn broke over the Yangtze River on their second day at anchor, thick fog still clung to everything. It stayed that way until late afternoon, when it began to dissipate. As the fog lifted, Hudson caught his first glimpse of China. They were anchored off a low-lying, grassy island surrounded by a shoreline that seemed to be made of muddy silt rather than sand. As darkness fell, the pilot decided the fog had thinned enough to begin the trip up the river. Hudson stood on deck and watched the moonlit land pass by as the *Dumfries* began the last leg of its journey. By the time they reached Woo-sung at the mouth of the Hwang-poo River, the fog had descended again, and they were forced to drop anchor once more.

Since Hudson was a passenger, the pilot arranged for him to be taken up the river to Shanghai on another pilot's junk. The small junk, with Hudson aboard, rocked back and forth but had little difficulty maneuvering in the fog. After several hours, it edged alongside a dock in Shanghai, and Hudson Taylor took his first step onto mainland China. It was Wednesday, March 1, 1854, and he had finally arrived. His feet were planted in China at last. He prayed a silent prayer, thanking God for His faithfulness in bringing him safely so far across the world.

The wharf was a bustle of activity, and around Hudson scurried Chinese men with plaitted queues bobbing from side to side as they made their way along. Most were wearing wide, cone-shaped straw hats, and some had bamboo poles over their shoulders. From the ends of the poles hung all sorts of things, from chickens and ducks to pails of liquid and baskets with eggs or grain in them. Hudson noticed two women. Their bound feet formed triangles at the bottoms of their legs, making them look more like horse's hooves than feet. The women seemed to fall forward, rather than walk, as they tottered slowly along the waterfront. All around him, Hudson could hear the lilting, singsong sound of Chinese being spoken.

As he looked at the sea of Chinese faces everywhere around him, Hudson felt terribly alone. More than two hundred thousand people lived in Shanghai, and not one of them was expecting him. All his belongings and every person he presently knew in China were still aboard the *Dumfries*, at anchor off Woo-sung. Unconsciously, he reached in and touched the letters of introduction in his vest pocket. Thank goodness he had friends who had friends in Shanghai.

He walked to the end of the dock, where he looked left. Sure enough, just as the pilot had told him, there was the British flag raised above a large, white building. It was the British Consulate, which, among other things, kept records of all the British subjects in and around the International Settlement. Hudson made his way to the building. He noticed as he did so that the ground seemed to rock back and forth beneath his feet. After five-and-a-half months on a ship at sea, it was going to take him a little while to get used to walking on land again.

He stopped in front of the building and looked up at Queen Victoria's coat of arms etched into the stone above the door. He swung the door open and stepped inside. Hudson was once again in a world with which he was familiar. He was standing in a room much like the lobby in the bank at Barnsley, only much, much bigger. In front of him was a large chart labeled "Ship Arrival and Departure Dates." He scanned the chart quickly; the *Dumfries* was penciled in under the column marked "Expected," but there was not yet any arrival date entered beside it. Hudson smiled to himself; he supposed not many passengers arrived before their ship.

Along the wall to his right was a counter. Above it hung a sign that read, "Royal Mail Received and Collected Here." On the counter was a smaller sign that said, "Closed until 9 A.M." Hudson's heart sank. He'd hoped to check for mail, especially letters from his family and from the Chinese Evangelization Society. The society had promised to have a letter of credit waiting for him. With the letter he would be able to go to the society's banking agent in Shanghai and withdraw some money. But it would have to wait until tomorrow. He didn't like the idea, though, of arriving at a stranger's house with little money, hoping they would offer him a bed for the night. But there was nothing he could do about it. He needed to get directions to the homes of the people named in his letters of introduction and make his way to visit them as fast as he could before dark.

He looked to his left. There was another counter with a sign above it that read, "General Enquiries." He introduced himself to the clerk behind the counter and took out the letters of introduction.

"Who is it you're looking for?" the clerk asked.

Hudson read the name off the front of the first envelope. "Pickering, Nicholas M."

The clerk pulled out a wooden file box and sorted through it. "No, that's not going to do you any good," he said, pulling a card from the box. He read from the card, "Departed Shanghai, January 28, aboard the *Sirene.* Destination, San Francisco.... Probably got the gold mining bug," he offered with a smile. "Anyone else?"

Hudson read the name from the next envelope. "Armstrong, Alfred B."

"Here he is, Alfred B." The clerk pulled another card from the box. "Oh dear," he said, pausing to take a deep breath. "You're not having much luck."

He flipped the card over so Hudson could read it. Across the top in large, red letters was stamped the single word "DECEASED," followed by the date, February 1, 1854.

"I am sorry about that," the clerk added with a sympathetic tone in his voice.

Hudson stared dumbly at the date. The man had died exactly one month ago. "What happened?" he asked.

"Typhus probably," replied the clerk. "It has gotten a lot of people lately. I would remember if it had been something to do with the fighting. Only lost a couple of people that way, in the wrong place at the wrong time. Bad luck really. But if the Imperial Army ever gets tired of shooting at the Red Turbans and turns their cannons on the International Settlement, boom, we're sitting ducks." He laughed nervously.

Appalled at what he had just heard, and down to his last hope, Hudson read the name from the front of the final envelope. "Dr. Walter Medhurst."

"Now that's a name I recognize. Everyone knows the Medhursts. They live in the London Missionary

Society compound," said the clerk enthusiastically, before going on to give Hudson directions for the two-mile walk to the compound.

Not far beyond the British Consulate, the streets turned to mud. Hudson picked his way along, trying to keep his feet as dry as possible until he came to the large, arched gateway to the compound. The gates were open, so Hudson went in. On one side was a building that looked like a hospital, and on the other side, several low houses. A Chinese servant was sweeping the open courtyard. He came running over as soon as he saw Hudson. He bowed three times and waited for Hudson to speak.

"Is Dr. Medhurst in? I have a letter of introduction for him," said Hudson.

The servant stared. Hudson could tell that he'd not understood a word. There was no one else in sight to ask, so he simplified his language and slowly tried again. "Me want Doctor Med-hurst."

A smile lit up the servant's eyes. "Doc-cor Me-hurse gone," he said, waving his hands toward the gate to underscore what he was saying.

Hudson's shoulders slumped. What did "gone" mean? The way things were turning out, gone could mean anything from out on an errand to dead!

"Where...has...Doctor...Medhurst...gone?" he asked slowly.

The servant beamed, evidently delighted his English had been understood. "Yes, gone," he said enthusiastically waving his arms again. "Gone."

Hudson stood wondering what to do. The apple trees at the back of the compound were casting long shadows across the courtyard. It would be dark soon, and he was beginning to wish he'd stayed on the *Dumfries* until she docked. As sunset approached, the air was getting cold, and the few shillings in his pocket surely would not be enough to pay for a night's lodging. Things looked bleak. Everyone he had an introduction to was either dead or gone.

He looked at the door to the hospital, wondering if there was anyone inside who might understand English. As if to answer his thoughts, the door swung open and out walked a European man. Seeing Hudson, he walked over and held out his hand. Relieved, Hudson shook it heartily.

"Edkins," he introduced himself in a strong English accent. "May I help you?"

Hudson handed him the letter of introduction. Edkins read it, then explained that Dr. Medhurst and his family had moved to a safer part of the city, since the compound was within earshot, and cannonshot, of the fighting. But Dr. Lockhart, Medhurst's partner, might be able to help him. Edkins showed Hudson into one of the nearby houses and went off to find Dr. Lockhart.

As Hudson waited, news of his arrival spread quickly. A procession of curious people stopped in to ask him who he was and what he was doing in China. How did he get here? No new ship had docked in the past week, had it? Were there other newcomers? Was he a doctor or a minister?

This last question proved the most difficult. When he said he was neither a doctor nor a minister, just a missionary, several people looked at him strangely. Someone even asked how a person could call himself a missionary without either correct church or medical training. It was a question that surprised Hudson, coming as it did from another missionary. It was also a question he would be asked over and over again during his stay in Shanghai.

Finally, Dr. Lockhart arrived. He welcomed Hudson and offered him a room in his house until he could get on his feet. Hudson was glad to take it, and after eating dinner with the Burdons, a young missionary couple at the compound, he went to bed. And for the first time in a long, long while, the bed wasn't rocking.

He was awakened a few hours later by bright flashes and the crash of cannonballs as they hit the nearby old city wall. The flashes lit up the bedroom, and the crashes made the oil lamp on the night-stand rattle. But soon Hudson grew used to the light and noise and fell asleep again.

He awoke to new sounds the next morning. "My pleasure in awakening and hearing the cheerful song of birds may be better imagined than described. The green corn waving in the fields, budding plants in the garden, and sweetly perfumed blossoms on some of the trees were indeed delightful after so long at sea," he wrote to Amelia in a letter. Of course, he did not tell her about the cannonfire during the night.

Things aren't so bad after all, he thought, as he pulled on his boots. He decided he would go back to the British Consulate and collect the letter of credit from the Chinese Evangelization Society and, he hoped, some other letters from family and friends back home. Then he would stroll along the river's edge keeping watch for the *Dumfries.* When she docked, he would unload his belongings and settle into his new room. It was a good plan but, as circumstances would have it, not one that worked.

Chapter 9

"If Only They Knew of the Living God"

Hudson walked out the compound gates and headed towards the Hwang-poo River. Dr. Lockhart's servant followed him at a distance. But eager as he was to reach the consulate office, Hudson couldn't help stopping along the way. Everything fascinated him. Shanghai was so different from London. Certainly London was busy, but Shanghai seemed so much busier. Even though the city was under siege, everywhere he looked there was activity. By the side of the muddy road was an old man making lanterns from red paper. Two boys were selling brightly colored birds in bamboo cages. Another man was selling oval-shaped, green fruit, unlike anything Hudson had seen before. A woman nursing a baby squatted beside a grass mat with cups of cooked rice arranged on it. Anyone who wasn't selling something seemed to be carrying something. As at the dock the day before, men were weaving in and out of the crowd, balancing bamboo poles across their shoulders. One man scurried by with live roosters tied by their feet dangling from his pole. Another man had embroidered silk pillows tied to his. Young men also went by pushing wheel-barrows loaded with huge clay pots filled with water. Everywhere there was the sound of people talking, laughing, and bartering. The air was also filled with interesting smells: the smell of food cooking in large woks over open fires, of live pigs and chickens and ducks, of the fragrant incense sold by merchants, and of the open sewers that ran alongside the street. The smells hung in the air, at times making Hudson want to breath deeply to savor them and at other times causing him to gag.

As he walked along, he wondered how he could describe the scene in his next letter to Amelia. The only thing he could think to compare it with was their visit to the Great Exhibition in London two years ago. But how orderly that had been compared to this!

Every few yards he stopped to examine some-thing for sale or to peer through a gate. But he was also eager to get the letter of credit from the Chinese Evangelization Society, along with his instructions on where and how to proceed in setting up the mission in Shanghai. He thought the first thing they would want him to do would be to find somewhere permanent to live while he prepared to go into the heart of China.

The British Consulate loomed in front of him once again. He climbed the steps to the consulate and entered, glancing behind at Dr. Lockhart's servant who was waiting on the bottom step. How nice it felt to be able to read all of the signs and charts and to know he spoke the same language as every other person in the room. There was a line at the mail counter, and Hudson found himself waiting behind a woman in a long, hooped dress that pinched in at her waist. Her dress would have been perfectly normal in London, but in Shanghai it looked strangely out of place and impractical for the crowded, muddy streets.

Finally, it was Hudson's turn to collect his mail. He said his name clearly and held out his hands, ready for the pile of letters. The clerk handed him only one letter. Hudson immediately recognized the handwriting on the envelope as his mother's. He waited for more letters. But instead of handing him more letters, the clerk said to him, "Two shillings please, there is insufficient postage on this letter. You owe the difference."

Hudson reached into his jacket pocket and handed two shillings to the clerk, who entered the amount in a ledger and stamped "paid" beside it.

Still Hudson waited patiently for more letters. The clerk looked puzzled. "That's it, sir," he said, before addressing the man standing in line behind him.

Hudson moved away from the mail counter with the words, "That's it, sir," ringing in his ears. That wasn't it. There was only one letter. The Burdons had told him a mail steamer came from England every month. They were much faster at making the trip from England than a sailing ship like the *Dumfries*. So how could it be that there was only one letter, and it wasn't from the Chinese Evangelization Society? Where was their letter of credit? He needed that letter, and he needed it now. *What did they expect him to do in China with no money and no instructions on how to proceed?*

A second thought flashed through his mind. *How do I keep the fact that I received no letter of credit from the other missionaries?* After only one night at the London Missionary Society compound, Hudson could sense that the other missionaries thought the Chinese Evangelization Society was a joke. What would they think when they found out the society had left him without money or instructions on what they wanted him to do?

Hudson was still stunned as he left the British Consulate and headed to the docks. The fog had cleared, and the sight of the *Dumfries* sailing up the river cheered him up. It had been only a day, but it seemed like such a long time since he had seen Captain Morris.

The *Dumfries* docked amid much yelling and arm waving. As soon as the pilot disembarked, Hudson was allowed aboard. Captain Morris was glad to see him and gave him a hearty handshake.

Then he ordered the crew to lower Hudson's baggage onto the dock.

Hudson was grateful that Dr. Lockhart had sent along his servant with instructions to help him get his belongings back to the compound. There was no way he could have made himself understood to the laborers, or coolies, as they were called, who hung around the dock. Dr. Lockhart's servant quickly hired seven coolies to transport Hudson's belongings to the compound. They busily tied his things to ropes, then suspended them from bamboo poles. The first coolie had Hudson's harmonium dangling on one end of his pole, balanced by several bundles of books on the other. Two of the other coolies had looped a rope through the handles of his sea chest and carried it suspended on a bamboo pole between them. The chest bounced up and down as they walked. Hudson led the procession of coolies through the streets back to the compound. As they moved along, they blended in with the clatter of activity going on around them.

It took Hudson only an afternoon to unpack his belongings and arrange them in his room. Unfortunately, his spare pair of shoes had been drenched on the voyage, probably when the hatch cover gave way during the storm in the Irish Sea, and so he had to discard them. He also had to discard a pile of his Bible study notes. Several ink bottles had broken and doused the pages in black ink so they couldn't be read. As he unpacked, he had plenty of time to think about what he should do next. He read his mother's letter over and over, hoping it would somehow give him an answer, but it didn't.

By Sunday afternoon, he was getting restless. No new mail steamers had arrived, and he was not sleeping well. The crash of cannonballs hitting their target was keeping him awake at night. So it was a great relief when Alexander Wylie, the London Missionary Society printer, offered to take Hudson on a tour of the old walled city.

The old city was surrounded on three sides by fifty thousand troops from the Imperial Army. On the fourth side lay the International Settlement. As they walked through the busy streets of the International Settlement towards the old city, Alexander Wylie explained that because of the Treaty of Nanking, the Imperial Army had no power over the International Settlement. They couldn't surround it or harm it in any way. The situation greatly frustrated the army because some foreigners, hoping to see them defeated, were helping the Red Turbans inside the old city. They were supplying them with food, armaments, and anything else that might give them an edge over the Imperial troops. With the rebels and the residents of old Shanghai receiving supplies and information about troop movements from foreigners, the siege could go on indefinitely. So naturally, the Imperial Army resented interfering foreigners.

As they stopped under the shade of a flowering plum tree for a rest, Hudson asked Alexander Wylie how the missionaries felt about the siege.

Wylie told him that the situation was a problem for missionaries. Missionaries tended to know the various Chinese dialects better than any other foreigners and so were constantly being asked to spy for both sides. Some did, while others acted as official translators. It was impossible not to be moved by the plight of starving people inside the old city. Yet everyone knew that giving them aid only kept the war going longer. There were no easy answers to the situation for the missionaries living in the International Settlement.

The two men made their way along the edge of a canal that led up to the walled city. The south gate was closed, so they began walking around the outside of the wall. Two minutes later they saw a ladder that had been hung over the wall.

"After you," said Alexander Wylie, gesturing for Hudson to climb the ladder.

Hudson grasped the bamboo and rope ladder with both hands and began to climb. At the top, he gazed down at the scene on the other side of the wall. As far as he could see, there were houses with their roofs either missing or damaged or with gaping holes in their walls. Some houses had simply been reduced to piles of charred wood and crumbled brick. Even the dirt streets had holes blown in them. In the middle of it all, people wandered around aimlessly. Hudson trembled as he climbed over the wall and down the ladder on the other side. It was one thing to hear the noises of war; it was quite another thing to see its destruction.

Alexander Wylie followed closely behind. The scene did not seem to bother him. Hudson supposed today seemed no more desperate to him than any other day. Together, they began walking in the direction of a Buddhist temple. Along the way, Wylie and Hudson gave out tracts. As they did so, Hudson prayed silently that they would be read before they were burned as fuel or wadded together to fill a hole in a wall. Alexander Wylie stopped often to talk with people, and Hudson envied the way he was able to slip from English to Chinese and back again.

Eventually they reached the Buddhist temple, where a yellow-robed priest greeted them. Inside the temple Hudson could see men and women burning incense and praying to a large stone statue of Buddha. Hudson watched intently. In all his life he had never seen anything other than a Christian church. And what struck him as he viewed the scene was not how different a Buddhist temple was from a Christian church, but the sincerity with which the worshippers worshipped a stone statue. *If only they knew of the living God,* he thought.

Still thinking about the Buddhist worshippers, Hudson followed Alexander Wylie to the north gate. As they got nearer to the gate they could hear shouting and screaming. Some kind of fight was in progress. Wylie put his hand out and stopped Hudson. It would be dangerous to go any closer to the fighting, he explained. But even if they did not go closer to the fighting, the results of the fighting were paraded right past them, as maimed and dead bodies were dragged away.

It was a relief to Hudson when they finally approached a London Missionary Society chapel and heard singing. They slipped quietly into the back of the chapel, where Dr. Medhurst had just begun to preach a sermon. Hudson concentrated hard on Dr. Medhurst's Chinese. It was so hard to pick out individual words as the sounds flowed together in what sounded more like singing than speaking. He looked around the chapel. One of its walls had a hole blown in it by a cannonball, and a pile of smashed chairs lay beside the hole.

After the service, the men talked with Dr. Medhurst, who agreed to meet them at the north gate in half an hour. Dr. Medhurst had some errands to run, and Alexander Wylie wanted to show Hudson some backstreets near the chapel.

They had walked a quarter of a mile when a group of yelling men with red turbans came into view. As they got closer, Hudson could see that they were pushing a small cannon. From the satisfied looks on their faces, he guessed they had just captured it from the Imperial Army. Behind them were five men, kicking and screaming, being dragged by their queues. It was plain from the uniforms they wore that they were Imperial Army soldiers. As soon as they saw Hudson and Alexander Wylie, they grabbed at their clothes. One of them got ahold of Hudson's trousers, but a Red Turban roughly jerked him away. Hudson did not need to understand their words to know they were begging for help; the pleading look in the their eyes said it all.

The two missionaries stood helpless as the group rounded a corner and disappeared from sight. There was nothing they could do for the men in the face of such a mob. Hudson asked Alexander Wylie what would happen to them. Wylie explained that they were captured soldiers on their way to be beheaded. He told Hudson that it was the most feared death a Chinese person could face, because they believed that if a person entered the afterlife without a head, he would have to live for eternity without one. That was why it was so hard to get a Chinese person to agree to an amputation, he added.

Hudson was still trying to put the picture of the pleading man out of his mind when they found a trail of fresh blood right where they had agreed to meet Dr. Medhurst. Fearing the worst, they followed the trail back to the International Settlement. Thankfully, Dr. Medhurst was unhurt, but he had quite a story to tell. While waiting for Hudson and Alexander Wylie, he had begun talking with two coolies. He heard cannon fire and so decided it would be best to walk on alone. He had walked about ten feet when a cannonball whistled over-head and landed right where he had been standing. The two coolies had their ankles smashed. Blood flowed from their legs as they were hurried to the hospital, explaining the trail of blood. The only hope of survival for either coolie was to amputate his legs, which they had both refused. All that could be done now was to make them comfortable as they awaited certain death.

The missionaries arrived back at the London Missionary Society compound, and Hudson went to his room, sobered by all he had seen. How different it all was from Sunday afternoons in England. He had prepared himself for many things in coming to China, but not for being in the middle of a war.

Worst of all, in the midst of all the suffering he had seen, he felt useless. Inside the old city men, women, and children were praying at shrines to their ancestors and stone idols, while he had the knowledge of the true and living God who could really answer their prayers. His heart burned to tell these people about God's love, but he didn't know how to speak a word of Chinese. If he was going to fulfill his burning desire to share the Gospel with the people of China, he was going to have to learn Chinese, and learn it fast.

The following morning, Dr. Medhurst suggested that Hudson start learning the Mandarin dialect of Chinese rather than the local dialect spoken around Shanghai. He explained that a mandarin was a government-appointed leader and magistrate. Every city had one, and it was his job to settle problems and rule the people according to the instructions he received from the emperor. It had been that way in China for many centuries, and it meant that a country as large as China was could be ruled quite efficiently. The mandarins, as well as the people of learning and many merchants in the country, spoke a dialect known as Mandarin. No matter what province they were from, they could all understand and talk to each other, and the emperor could easily communicate to the mandarins how he wanted them to rule.

Hudson could see the wisdom of Dr. Medhurst's suggestion. By learning the Mandarin dialect, he would be able to communicate with people wherever he went, even deep in the heart of China.

Dr. Medhurst arranged for a tutor to teach Hudson Mandarin, so each morning the tutor and Hudson spent several hours studying the dialect. Hudson proved to be a fast learner, and much to everyone's surprise, it wasn't long before he was going to the market on his own and bartering in Mandarin with the merchants over the price of his purchases.

Dr. Medhurst could see a lot of promise in Hudson as a doctor, and since it seemed to him that the Chinese Evangelization Society had no real plan for him, he invited Hudson to continue his medical studies at the London Missionary Society hospital.

Hudson accepted the invitation, and soon his days were divided between learning the Mandarin dialect and caring for patients at the hospital.

He was busy, yes, but still not fulfilled. He was in China, but only on the coastal plain. He wanted to be moving inland, but first he needed money and instructions from the Chinese Evangelization Society. Why was it taking them so long?

Chapter 10

One of the Crowd

The other missionaries watched Hudson closely. The Chinese Evangelization Society was a new organization, and they wanted to see how it cared for its only worker. And what they saw was not impressive. To them, the society had sent out an unqualified, unmarried man, without any instructions as to what they wanted him to do and, judging by his clothes and the food he ate, with very little income. What were they thinking?

After several months, Hudson was beginning to wonder the same thing. He became more and more lonely. He didn't dare tell anyone how difficult things really were for him; doing so would only give the other missionaries more reason to criticize the Chinese Evangelization Society.

Finally, letters did begin to arrive from the society. Hudson received his letter of credit and was able to arrange to get some money to pay his expenses. But the money was never enough. The society paid him a salary of eighty pounds per year, from which he had to meet all his expenses. Single missionaries with the London Missionary Society were paid seven hundred pounds a year, as well as having their rent and other expenses paid. Hudson wrote to the Chinese Evangelization Society and explained to them how the war had driven up the price of everything in Shanghai. He asked if they could possibly increase the amount of money they paid him, in light of the increased costs. The letter he received back was not what he expected.

Instead of increasing Hudson's salary, the society announced that it was sending another missionary to work in Shanghai, and not just a single person like Hudson, but a man with a wife and two children. In fact, Dr. Parker and his family were already on their way on a ship called the *Swiftsure*.

Hudson wanted to feel delighted at the thought of having another missionary from the Chinese Evangelization Society with him in Shanghai, but mostly he was filled with a sense of dread. As usual, the society had sent no instructions on how they wanted him to prepare for Dr. Parker's arrival. He supposed they would want him to rent a house that they could all live in and set up as society headquarters in China. But he kept telling the society in his letters back to them in London that there was not a house to be rented in the whole International Settlement because of the siege. Hudson was twenty-one years old, barely able to survive on his meager income, and now he also had to be responsible for a whole family in a city where not a house or room was available for rent. He wondered how much the Chinese Evangelization Society had told the Parkers about conditions in Shanghai. When they arrived, would they be as surprised at the conditions as he'd been?

Hudson had eaten his first meal in China with the Burdons, a young couple with the London Missionary Society. The Burdons and Hudson had become good friends and spent much time together. Now Mrs. Burdon lay dying of cholera. Hudson spent long hours at the Burdons' house caring for Mrs. Burdon; her husband, John, who was also ill; and their three-month-old baby daughter. Finally, on September 26, Mrs. Burdon died, and with great sorrow, Hudson made the arrangements for her funeral service and burial. Slowly, John Burdon regained his strength, and at the end of October, he decided to move out of his house and in with the London Missionary Society's chaplain, whose wife was going to help him look after his small daughter. John Burdon offered to rent the house to Hudson, who gladly accepted.

It was now mid-November, and each morning Hudson walked to the docks to see if there was news of the *Swiftsure*'s arrival. When there was no word on its arrival after many days, he began to wonder if it had been shipwrecked. He was even more anxious after he heard the news that the *Dumfries* had been wrecked on the return voyage to England, though thankfully Captain Morris and his crew had been saved.

Finally, on November 27, 1854, two weeks late, the *Swiftsure* sailed up the Hwang-poo River to Shanghai. The ship docked, and Hudson greeted the Parkers warmly. To his surprise, although the Parkers left England with two children, they arrived in Shanghai with three. Mrs. Parker had given birth during the voyage.

Hudson arranged for some coolies to carry their baggage, and nine months after he'd made the same trek himself, he led them all through the streets of the International Settlement to the London Mission Society compound.

At the compound, he showed the Parkers to the new headquarters of the Chinese Evangelization Society. Even with Hudson's belongings spread around the house, it looked empty. There was little furniture in the house, because all Hudson's money had gone towards paying the rent. Buying furniture had to wait.

The next morning, Hudson and Dr. Parker, an independent-minded Scotsman, went down to the British Consulate to collect the mail. Dr. Parker had been told that the Chinese Evangelization Society would have a letter of credit waiting for him when he arrived. And just as Hudson had been, Dr. Parker was shocked when no such letter was waiting for him. It was a familiar story by now to Hudson.

It was good, though, having a fellow worker in the mission. Hudson and Dr. Parker would sit and talk and scheme and plan late into the evening. Yet despite the company, Hudson felt gloomy. He'd been in China nearly a year now, and he was still stuck in Shanghai. He ached to be able to start moving inland. But with the war and the hostile attitude towards foreigners, there was little he could do until the situation changed. And of course, he was the "most experienced" missionary in the Chinese Evangelization Society, and with that came the responsibility for taking care of the Parkers. It was ironic. Here in Shanghai, the heart of China seemed further from Hudson's reach than it ever had back in England.

Finally, in February 1855, Hudson got some good news. Alexander Wylie and John Burdon had managed to organize permits that would allow them to travel inland for one week, and they wanted Hudson to go with them.

On the second day of their trip, they decided to hold a worship service on top of a hill from which they could see Shanghai far off in the distance. It was a beautiful spot, and they were soon lost in thanking God for His wonderful creation and for allowing them the privilege of being His servants in

China. As they worshipped, Hudson glanced in the direction of Shanghai and saw a huge cloud of smoke rising from the city. It could mean only one thing: Shanghai had fallen to the Imperial Army. But at what cost? The three men abandoned their trip and hurried back to Shanghai, not knowing what they would find. As they made their way back, they passed fleeing people who told the three missionaries that rather than give up, the Red Turbans had blown up the south gate and set fire to the city. The Imperial Army had then entered the city and begun killing people. It was a bloodbath, and the terror of it was written on the faces of those fleeing.

When they reached the city, they found it just as they had been told. There were bodies everywhere. It seemed as though there wasn't a house or building in the whole city that wasn't burned. Death and destruction were everywhere. Looking at the scene made Hudson feel sick.

Fortunately, except for the damage of a few stray cannonballs, the International Settlement escaped unscathed.

That night, for the first time since Hudson had arrived in China, the city of Shanghai was silent. There were no bombs, no explosions. There was only the silence of death.

The missionaries worked hard in the following weeks, ministering to those who had survived the slaughter. And slowly from the rubble a new Shanghai began to rise.

Since their earlier trip had been cut short, Hudson and John Burdon decided to make another one. This time they would head for Tung-chow, farther up the Yangtze River. Tung-chow was also known as "Satan's Seat," because the people of the city were so lawless and hard to control. There was so much crime in the city that most Chinese people chose to avoid it altogether.

They hired two small junks and headed up the river. When they reached the dock, the captains of the two junks became very worried about Hudson and John Burdon's safety. Surely they had heard of the city's reputation? So Hudson thought of an escape plan. If he and John Burdon did not return by nightfall, one junk was to go back down river to Shanghai as quickly as possible with the news they had been captured. The other junk would anchor near the dock just in case the two men managed to escape.

With their plan made, both men slept soundly and packed their bags at first light.

The city of Tung-chow was actually a distance from the dock on the river, so Hudson, John Burdon, and a servant began the walk to town. The road, though, was very rough, and they had to walk slowly. Finally they decided it would be quicker to hire wheelbarrows and pushers to take them to Tung-chow. Wheelbarrows were a common form of transportation in China. They were large enough so that a man could sit in one with room left over for baggage. They hired three wheelbarrows and loaded themselves in, along with the Chinese Bibles and tracts they were carrying, and held on for the ride.

The wheelbarrow pushers knew every bump in the road and guided their barrows around most of them. As they bounced along, the servant who was accompanying them had time to think about where he was going and with whom. Finally, when someone spat at him for traveling with "foreign devils," it became too much for him. He yelled for the wheelbarrow pushers to stop and begged Hudson and John Burdon to let him return to the junks. Seeing how scared he was, the two missionaries agreed.

They were getting close to the city when an important-looking man motioned for them to stop. He spoke to them in Mandarin and begged both of them to turn around. Tung-chow was not a safe place for foreigners, and he didn't think they deserved to die there.

The man walked on, but now the wheelbarrow pushers were unwilling to go any farther. They were convinced the "foreign devils" riding in their wheelbarrows would be attacked and killed, and if they were in the way, they might be killed too. So they ordered Hudson and John Burdon out and jogged off with their barrows in the opposite direction.

Hudson found two new wheelbarrow pushers willing to take them into the city, but they demanded to be paid "danger money" for their effort. Eventually, without their servant, and with new pushers, Hudson and John Burdon found themselves entering the west gate of Tung-chow.

They climbed out of their wheelbarrows. Dust and sweat had mixed together to form little rivers of mud that ran down their necks and dripped from their brows. Hudson pulled some Bibles from his bag and began asking people if they could read. If a person said he could, he gave him a Bible and explained that it was God's message to him. Several people thanked him. Things seemed to be going quietly, but not for long. A huge, drunken man pushed his way to the front of the crowd that had gathered around the two men, grabbed Hudson by the throat, and began choking him. Hudson gasped and spluttered and tried to pry the man's hand off his throat.

John Burdon began yelling, "We demand to be taken to the mandarin."

The drunken man loosened his grip on Hudson. "We know what to do with you!" he sneered.

A roar went up from the crowd, and people began poking at the two missionaries with sticks. "Kill the foreign devils," they began to chant.

By now, Hudson's captor was dragging him along by the neck. Another two men were dragging John Burdon. Even so, John Burdon was able to reach into his bag and throw out tracts to the people.

Throwing out tracts, though, annoyed many people in the mob. They began jabbing their sticks at the two missionaries with greater force than before.

"Remember how the apostles rejoiced that they were counted worthy to suffer in the cause of Christ," Hudson yelled back to John Burdon in English.

The huge, drunken man tightened his grip on Hudson's throat so he could say no more. Hudson had to do something, but what? He remembered his identity card in the left pocket of his pants. Slowly, he slid his hand down into the pocket. He could feel the card. Quickly he grabbed it and waved it in the air.

"I demand to be taken to the mandarin," he yelled.

The sight of an official identity card quieted the mob. The card meant the two men they were dragging along probably had important friends. Perhaps it would be better to take them to the mandarin after all, they decided.

Hudson slumped down in front of the mandarin's house, totally exhausted. His throat burned, and his whole body felt out of joint. The ringleaders of the mob went inside to talk to the mandarin. The rest of the mob crowded in around the two of them. John Burdon, though, saw a great opportunity. Here was a large crowd who had never heard about Jesus. He propped himself up against a wall for support and began preaching to the crowd.

A few minutes later, the mandarin's servants came out and dragged Hudson and John Burdon inside the gates. They pulled the two of them to their feet and told them they were going to see Ch'en Ta Lao-ie (the Great Venerable Grandfather Ch'en), the mandarin of Tung-chow.

Hudson and John Burdon were led into a room filled with polished wood furniture and painted silk pictures. The Great Venerable Grandfather Ch'en sat on a cushioned chair at the far end of the room.

The mandarin welcomed them both. He took them into a private room and offered them some tea. Hudson was glad to drink it, as it soothed his throat. Grandfather Ch'en explained to them that he knew many things. He had been an official in Shanghai and knew about the Treaty of Nanking, and that foreigners were not to be treated roughly. He asked what they were doing in Tung-chow, and since Hudson spoke the better Mandarin, he answered Ch'en's questions. He explained that they were bringing the truth of God to the people of the city, and how they had not meant to cause a disturbance. He also explained that the crowd had not treated them kindly and that he hoped things might go more smoothly from now on.

The mandarin nodded. He was glad the visitors had not complained about his citizens, like most foreigners would. These were foreigners who knew some Chinese manners.

Hudson asked the Great Venerable Grandfather Ch'en if he could leave a Bible for him to read and if they could give out the rest of their Bibles and tracts in the town.

The mandarin nodded his head. And more, he even provided them with an escort so they would not be disturbed again.

This time, out on the streets, Hudson and John Burdon were treated as important guests of the mandarin. If people did not move out of the way quickly enough and let them through, their escorts used their long queues as whips to clear the way. So, with the protection of the mandarin's pigtail-whipping guards, the two missionaries gave out the last of their tracts and Bibles.

Much to everyone's surprise, the missionaries arrived back at the junks in one piece and before dark.

During the next year, Hudson, accompanied by various other missionaries, made several more trips inland from Shanghai. He also took a trip down the coast to another of the treaty ports, Ning-po. Dr. Parker accompanied him on that trip. There were many missionaries working in Ning-po, and there were also lots of foreign merchants and officials. But in all the city, there was no medical clinic or doctor. Hudson and Dr. Parker prayed and talked about the opportunity that existed. Finally, they decided that Dr. Parker and his family should move to Ning-po and set up a hospital.

As Hudson made his trips inland, he wrestled with a problem. What Wilhelm Lobscheid had told him four years before at the meeting in London was true. Even when he was only ten or twenty miles from Shanghai, he scared people. They were not used to his foreign clothes, polished shoes, or curly blond hair. He remembered that to blend in, Dr. Medhurst had dressed in Chinese clothing when he made his earlier trips into inland China. So he spoke to Dr. Medhurst about the situation, and the doctor encouraged Hudson to start wearing Chinese clothing.

His wearing Chinese clothes might make Chinese people happy, but Hudson had a feeling it would make many of the other missionaries angry. They thought they were "civilizing" the Chinese, and an Englishman dressed in Chinese clothing had things completely the wrong way 'round. Besides, looking British was a protection. Everyone knew that to harm a person dressed in English clothes was to insult the powerful British Empire.

But as Hudson thought about it, he became convinced there were more good points than bad to dressing like the Chinese. And not only dressing like them but looking like them as well. He hired a barber who cut off the blond curls that hung on his forehead. Then the barber shaved the front half of Hudson's head. The razor made a few small cuts in his scalp that stung when the barber smeared black hair dye on his remaining hair. Once the dying was complete, the barber braided a false queue into his newly blackened curls.

Next Hudson bought himself some Chinese clothes and put them on. He started with the pants, which were enormous. The waist seemed twice as wide as he was. The merchant was right, one size definitely did fit all. Fortunately, the men wore their pants with a belt. So he put the belt on and bunched the top of the pants inside it. Next he put on socks. They felt scratchy on his feet, and they had no elastic at the top. The legs of his oversized pants were tucked into the socks, and two very strong garters were used to hold the pants down and the socks up. He put on a plain cotton shirt, over which an embroidered tunic was then pulled. This tunic reached all the way to Hudson's feet, hiding his baggy pants. The sleeves of the tunic hung eighteen inches below his fingertips. Every time he wanted to do something with his hands, he had to remember to roll the sleeves up, then fold them down again afterwards. It seemed quite impractical to Hudson, but that was how Chinese men wore them. The shoes, though, proved the most difficult to get on. He had to fold his socks against his feet and then maneuver the cloth shoes over the top of them. The shoes were designed to curl up at the toes, and the curls kept catching on the bottom of his tunic. Hudson looked at himself in the mirror. He was now a blue-eyed Chinaman.

Even so, it took a while before he was brave enough to walk outdoors in his new outfit. But when he did, he discovered that people didn't give him a second glance. After being so different for so long, it was strange to walk past a Chinese person without being stared at, or to not draw a crowd when he stopped to buy fruit in the market. For the first time since he left London, he really felt like one of the crowd.

Chapter 11

The Luckiest Man Alive

Each week, Dr. Medhurst held a prayer meeting in his home. Hudson regularly attended the meeting, as did William Burns, a Presbyterian minister from England who had made several trips inland with Hudson. On one particularly cold, wintry night, Captain Bowers, captain of the *Geelong*, a coastal sailing ship that serviced the treaty ports dotted up and down the coast of China, was attending the prayer meeting. He asked for prayer for the city of Swatow, eight hundred miles to the south. The captain had just come from there and could not forget the awful things he'd seen. Swatow was not a treaty port, but there were many foreigners living there. Most were traders: traders of opium, slaves, and prostitutes. Captain

Bowers wanted the group to pray that a missionary would feel called there.

Hudson couldn't get out of his mind all Captain Bowers had said about Swatow. He felt sure God was calling him to go. There was just one problem. He and William Burns had become close friends. Hudson hated the idea of leaving his friend. Indeed, they had become a very effective team, ministering together. But despite his personal feelings, Hudson had to obey God. So he went to tell William Burns his decision. When Hudson finally said he was leaving, a big smile spread across William Burns's face. That very evening, he had been going to tell Hudson exactly the same thing. God had called him to Swatow as well.

In March 1856, with free passage on the *Geelong*, the two men set out on their journey south. The ship stayed close to the coastline, and as they got farther south, they could see the plants and trees become more and more tropical. Apple trees were replaced by banana trees, and the fertile river plain that surrounded Shanghai slowly became steep mountains, whose sides had been terraced to grow rice. Silt and mud gave way to long, white sandy beaches. It was all so warm and bright and lush compared to Shanghai in winter.

In Swatow the two men rented an attic room above an incense shop. It was a big room that ran the length of the store. To get to it they had to climb a ladder propped behind the counter. There was no trapdoor to the room, and anytime someone in the shop was curious about what the foreign devils were doing, they just climbed the ladder and looked in.

Hudson learned some of the local dialect, and before long he was preaching in the streets. He and William Burns also set up a small medical clinic. Soon the clinic was bustling with people. Hudson did his best to meet their needs, but he had left most of his medicines, surgical equipment, and books back in Shanghai. For the clinic to be more effective, it was decided that Hudson should make an extended trip back to Shanghai and collect his things.

Someone in Shanghai could have saved him the trip if he had been told that a fire in the London Missionary Society store house had destroyed all his medical supplies. But since no one had written him, it was a great shock to Hudson when he reached Shanghai. Although discouraged and frustrated by what had happened to his belongings, he decided that after traveling eight hundred miles, he was not going to return empty-handed. So he set out for Ning-po to see if Dr. Parker had any spare supplies.

When he arrived, he found the new hospital nearly finished. Glad to see him, Dr. Parker asked Hudson to help him get things organized. There was much to do. Hudson decided the experience would be useful to him when he returned to Swatow.

It was two months before everything was organized. Hudson felt great satisfaction as the new hospital opened and began ministering to the medical needs of the local population. The two months had also given him a good opportunity to get to know John Jones and his wife Mary, who were the latest missionaries the Chinese Evangelization Society had sent to China. John Jones and Hudson became good friends. They made several short trips together to some of the outlying settlements around Ning-po to preach the Gospel and distribute tracts and Bibles.

Hudson made another friendship during his two months in Ning-po. Every Wednesday evening, the Parkers had dinner with Miss Aldersey and the Dyer sisters. At sixty years of age, Miss Aldersey was a formidable woman. She had been in China a long time and had single-handedly established a large school and orphanage, the first of its kind to be opened in China by Protestants. When Miss Aldersey made up her mind about something, there was no going back. She decided once that an early morning walk was good for her health. So at exactly 5 A.M. every morning she could be seen walking once around the city wall. If it snowed, she wore more clothes. If it was dark or foggy, a servant walked in front of her carrying a lantern. Nothing got in the way of her morning walk.

Many Chinese people found it difficult to imagine the mighty British Empire being run by a woman, Queen Victoria. Those who knew Miss Aldersey did not find it strange at all.

The Dyer sisters, twenty-one-year-old Brunella and nineteen-year-old Maria, came to be in Ning-po through a very roundabout set of circumstances.

The girls had been born in Singapore, where their parents were early missionaries with the London Missionary Society. When their father died, their mother married Mr. Bausum. He became the girls' stepfather. Not long after that, their mother died, and Mr. Bausum remarried. The girls continued to live with him and his new wife. Several years later, Mr. Bausum also died. After his death, the girls' uncle, William Tarn, who lived in London, became their guardian. He paid for their education, but the girls remained close to Mrs. Bausum, who, even though she had not known either of their parents, was like a mother to them.

Since she was getting on in age, Miss Aldersey had asked Mrs. Bausum to come to China and prepare to take over the management of the orphanage and school from her. Brunella and Maria agreed to go with her to China. That was how both girls came to be living in Ning-po.

During the time the girls had been in Ning-po, Miss Aldersey had given more and more of the control of the orphanage and school over to Mrs. Bausum. And having more spare time on her hands, she had taken more and more control over what Maria and Brunella did. In her mind, they were fragile young women in a land where men might take advantage of them. They had to be protected, and she was going to do it.

For that reason, Miss Aldersey was not pleased when Dr. Parker asked if he could bring Hudson along to dinner at her house. She could have said no, but that would have been bad manners. Yet to her, Hudson Taylor was an embarrassment to have around. He was short, had dyed hair and a ridiculous queue, and wore threadbare Chinese clothes. "Really," she asked the girls one evening after he had left the house, "does he have no pride in being British?"

For his part, Hudson enjoyed the evenings at Miss Aldersey's. Brunella and Maria both sang beautifully, and the food was always English, reminding him of his mother's cooking. He was completely unaware, though, of the effect he was having on one of the two sisters. While Miss Aldersey disliked Hudson more and more with each visit, tall, slim, brown-haired Maria saw him as more exciting and daring than anyone she had ever met.

Once the hospital was up and running, Hudson prepared to return to Swatow and his work with William Burns. Dr. Parker gave him as much medicine and equipment as he could spare, and Hudson set out for Shanghai, where another ship would take him down the coast to Swatow. When he got to Shanghai, there was an urgent letter waiting for him from William Burns. Burns had decided to take a trip inland from Swatow. In the course of the journey, he and his two servants had been arrested by Chinese authorities and put in jail in Canton. Eventually, he had been freed and turned over to the British Consul. But now the British Consul had forbidden them to return to Swatow and continue their work there. So there was no point in Hudson's returning.

Hudson was stunned. It had taken him three months of travel and work to get the medicine and equipment he needed for his clinic there. Besides, he enjoyed the work in Swatow. He'd looked forward to getting back there. There was so much to do, so many needs, both medical and spiritual, to be ministered to. What would happen to the people of Swatow without them?

As he thought about the situation, he decided he had two options while he waited to see if things changed in Swatow so that he could go back. He could either stay on in Shanghai or go back to Ning-po and work with Dr. Parker. He decided on going back to Ning-po.

Dr. Parker welcomed him back. Hudson moved into a house on Bridge Street, named for the bridge at each end of the street. Dr. Parker used the house as a school, but the attic was too cold for the children. That was where Hudson slept. On very cold winter mornings, it wasn't unusual for him to wake up and find a thin layer of snow on top of his quilt that had drifted in through the cracks in the tile roof.

Hudson fit right back into work at the hospital with Dr. Parker. And with John Jones, he also continued to preach in and around Ning-po.

The weeks quickly rolled by, and soon it was Christmas. Everyone tried to have fun, because in the back of everyone's mind was the thought that this could be the last Christmas spent together in Ning-po. Even as they danced and sang, the threat of another Opium War was never far from their thoughts.

The latest situation had started when the *Arrow*, which was actually a Chinese ship flying the British flag, was boarded and opium was found. The *Arrow*'s crew were dragged off and imprisoned by Chinese officials. The British were furious. How dare Chinese officials board a ship flying the Union Jack? Actually, the Chinese had every right to board the ship, since the *Arrow* had no right to be flying the British flag in the first place. The British, though, didn't worry too much about that. To them it was the Chinese trying to interfere with their trade again. And it had to stop. The British demanded an immediate apology or they would bomb Canton. When the Chinese didn't apologize, the British lit their cannons and bombarded the city.

Many foreigners, including Hudson, sided with the Chinese point of view. The British needed to remember that they were guests in a foreign country. But to the Chinese, all foreigners were the same. Some Chinese groups even offered to pay a bounty for the head of every foreign devil brought to them.

This put all foreigners in China in a very difficult position. In Hong Kong, a baker put arsenic in his bread and sold the loaves only to foreigners. Thankfully, he didn't use quite enough arsenic, and while many people got sick from eating the bread, no one died. In Ning-po itself, a group of Portuguese merchants were attacked and killed. Many missionaries were beginning to think they should leave Ning-po; China didn't seem to be a safe place any more.

The missionaries knew they were most likely to be attacked when they were all in one group, but they continued to meet for church and prayer meetings anyway. What they didn't know was that a band of angry Chinese men had asked the local magistrate for permission to kill all the missionaries in Ning-po. The magistrate had given his permission, and all that remained was to wait for the missionaries to gather for church on Sunday. It was arranged that the largest group of men would attack the church service, while a smaller group would round up and kill any missionary who wasn't at church.

One of the men planning the attack had a friend who worked for a missionary. He knew that when they carried out their plan, his friend might well be killed along with the foreigners, so he warned him of the attack. The man then told the missionary that employed him about the plan. News spread quickly among the missionaries. They decided to pray about the situation and called a special prayer meeting.

At the same time, a junior mandarin heard about the plan to kill the missionaries and went to the magistrate. He pointed out that if all the missionaries in the city were killed, it would anger foreigners so much that Ning-po would be attacked just as Canton had been. He pointed out that the British had the power to kill every Chinese person in Ning-po and level every building in return for the attack. The magistrate had not thought about this, and when he did, it scared him. He quickly sent out an order canceling the attack.

The prayers of the missionaries had been answered. But even though their lives had been spared this time, things were still very tense in Ning-po. Some missionaries hired bodyguards, but what was to stop the bodyguards from killing the missionaries?

Finally, it was decided that the women and children should go back to Shanghai and wait there until things settled down in Ning-po. Hudson and John Jones were asked to escort them.

The Dyer sisters, though, refused to go. They felt they needed to stay behind and help Mrs. Bausum keep the orphanage and school open.

Two boats were hired to take the women and children to Shanghai. As they sailed up the Grand Canal away from Ning-po, Hudson had the strangest thought. He wondered whether he would ever see Maria again.

Back in Shanghai, he couldn't get Maria out of his mind. So finally he wrote a letter to her and asked if she would be willing to get to know him better, with the possibility that they might one day get married.

Maria was thrilled to get Hudson's letter. She hadn't even been sure he knew she cared about him. But her joy was over when she told Miss Aldersey about the letter. Miss Aldersey was shocked. How dare Hudson Taylor, the silly little man parading himself around like a Chinaman, think he could marry one of "her" girls. He could barely support himself. What hope did he have of supporting Maria or making her happy? Such a marriage would be an embarrassment. It was unthinkable, and she was going to make sure it never happened.

She immediately wrote a letter to Mr. Tarn, Maria's uncle and guardian in London, and warned him that some undesirable missionary had fallen in love with his niece. Having written that letter, she called Maria into her study and made her write a letter telling Hudson she did not want to marry him and asking him never to mention the subject again.

Hudson was disappointed by Maria's letter, but even he'd begun to wonder exactly what he had to offer a wife. He put the letter aside and turned his attention to another troubling matter.

Since being in Shanghai, Hudson and John Jones had discovered that the Chinese Evangelization Society was borrowing the money they were sending to their missionaries. This worried both men. Hudson did not believe in borrowing for himself, and he found it difficult to accept someone else borrowing for him. He and John Jones prayed about what they should do. Finally, they both decided they should resign from the Chinese Evangelization Society.

Hudson now had no missionary society backing him and no other source of income. He was alone and was relying on God to meet all his needs, just as he had done in Hull and London.

While in Shanghai, Hudson also thought a lot about the challenge foreign missionaries faced in China, and he came to a conclusion: China was not going to be reached with the Gospel if the job was left to foreigners alone. There were too many difficulties to be overcome. The best thing for foreigners to do was train Chinese people to take the Gospel deep into China to their own people.

Hudson shared his insights with John Jones, and the two of them decided that when they got back to Ning-po they would throw their energy into starting a church in the house on Bridge Street, where they could train up Chinese Christians to go and share the Gospel.

After two months in Shanghai, the situation in Ning-po settled down, and the women and children were able to return.

After he got back, Hudson would sometimes see Maria at a friend's house, but they did not speak to each other more than they had to. But as he continued to think about things with Maria, Hudson wondered if Miss Aldersey might be at the bottom of Maria's letter of rejection. So he decided to pay her a visit. It was not a pleasant visit, but he did find out that she had made Maria write the letter to him. He also found out a few other things. Miss Aldersey made it very clear to him that she did not think he was fit to ask anyone to be his wife. Her comments reminded him of the letter from Marianne's father three years earlier.

After his visit, things got worse for him. Miss Aldersey started rumors around the community about Hudson. But despite her efforts, Hudson would not give up. He had to know how Maria felt about him. The opportunity to ask her came not long afterwards, when there was a women's prayer meeting at the Bridge Street church. Hudson had gone out for the evening so as not to disturb the women. When he returned, he saw that not all the women had left. His heart beat faster. He opened the door, and sure enough, Maria was still there, sitting by the window. Mrs. Bausum sat beside her, but Miss Aldersey had already left. This was Hudson's chance. He asked Mrs. Bausum if he could talk with Maria, and soon the three of them were alone in one of the upstairs rooms. Hudson pretended Mrs. Bausum was not there, as he told Maria that he loved her. Maria smiled and nodded; she loved Hudson, too. Within minutes, things were settled. Hudson would write to Mr. Tarn and ask his permission to marry Maria.

When Miss Aldersey found out that Maria and Hudson had met and talked together, she was furious. She wrote Hudson a rude letter, telling him he ought to be ashamed to call himself a Christian, going around luring young missionary girls who did not know any better. But all her ranting did no good. Mr. Tarn wrote back and gave his permission for Hudson and Maria to be married. And so they were.

On January 20, 1858, one year after Hudson had taken the women and children away from Ning-po to safety in Shanghai, he was standing at the front of a church with Maria, who wore a gray silk dress with a long wedding veil. He, himself, had freshly dyed his queue and bought a new suit of Chinese clothes for the wedding. As he stood at the front of the church, he felt that he was the luckiest man alive to have such a beautiful bride.

Hudson and Maria had their honeymoon in a wonderful old monastery in the hills overlooking Ning-po. They were very happy together. Unfortunately, after only two weeks of marriage, Maria became very ill. She had typhoid, a disease that was often deadly. Hudson took care of her, but just as she was beginning to get better, Hudson came down with the disease himself. Mrs. Bausum kindly looked after them both, and it was April before Hudson and Maria were well enough to move into the Bridge Street house together. Indeed, it would be many years before Hudson was completely well again.

A year went by, and Hudson continued to work hard at establishing a church in the Bridge Street house while Maria opened a small school for girls.

Those were happy times for Hudson and Maria, but during the second year of their marriage, some changes took place. In July a baby daughter was born. They named her Grace Dyer Taylor. She was a pretty little girl, and everyone loved to make her laugh.

The next change was a sad one. In August, Dr. Parker's wife became ill with cholera and died within two days. Everyone was stunned by her sudden death, and Dr. Parker was too upset to go on with his medical work. He decided to take their four children back to Scotland, where his parents could help him raise them.

But who would run the hospital he had labored so hard to establish? There was no other qualified doctor in all of Ning-po to take it over. The hospital would have to close. But what about the dispensary? Here, all eyes fell on Hudson. It wasn't possible for him to keep it open, Hudson protested. Dr. Parker treated private, foreign patients to make money to keep the hospital and dispensary open. Since Hudson was not a qualified doctor, he couldn't do that.

Still, he agreed to consider it, and he and Maria fasted and prayed. After several days, Hudson felt that he should take over not only the dispensary but also the hospital. Somehow, with God's help, they would make it work.

Dr. Parker left them with enough money to run the hospital for a month, and then, eight days after burying his wife, he left for Scotland.

The hospital turned out to be a wonderful place for the Chinese Christians from the Bridge Street church to learn how to serve each other. The church had decided that the hospital should be its project. Members of the congregation worked day after day at the hospital without pay. They cleaned and washed, sang and preached. Hudson could not have been happier than to see the Chinese people he had trained reaching out to others.

But they still needed money to run the hospital. Everyone watched eagerly as the money ran out. They wondered if Hudson was right. Would God send more money?

The situation became serious. A year and a half earlier, Hudson didn't know if he could support a wife, and now he had a wife, a child, and a hospital to pay for.

One afternoon, the cook, who was a new convert, came to tell Hudson he had just opened their last bag of rice. At the same moment, the mail arrived. In it was a letter from a Mr. Berger in England and a check for fifty pounds. If Hudson needed more money, Mr. Berger instructed in his letter, he just needed to write and say how much more, and the amount would be sent to him. Hudson read the letter to the cook, who ran yelling down the hallway of the hospital, "God answers prayer, God answers prayer."

In the following months, there were many other wonderful answers to prayer that allowed the hospital to keep on ministering to people's needs. The

Bridge Street church also grew to twenty-one active members, and there were lots of other people who were interested in knowing more about the Gospel. Every afternoon, Hudson taught new converts how to read the Bible and follow its teaching. But every afternoon, he found it a little more difficult to concentrate. He did not like to admit it to himself, but he was becoming a very sick man.

Chapter 12

In the Light of Eternity

Hudson, Maria cuddling Grace in her arms, and Wang Lae-djun, a Chinese Christian from the Bridge Street church, stood together on the deck of the *Jubilee*, a speedy new clipper ship. The water slowly turned from yellow to blue as the ship cleared the Yangtze Delta and headed for the open waters of the China Sea. Hudson strained for his last look at China. His heart was so heavy he could not speak. There was still so much to do for God in China, but he could not stay; his body had betrayed him. After six years in China, at age twenty-eight, he had contracted tuberculosis. After putting off consulting the doctor for several months, Hudson had finally sought him out, even though he knew what the doctor would tell him. He should return

147

home to England immediately, where good food, the best doctors, and a cooler climate would help him overcome the disease. And if he didn't return home, most likely he would die in a matter of months.

The *Jubilee* made the trip back to England in only four months, which was a good thing, because one-year-old Grace screamed with teething most of the trip, and Maria got gastroenteritis, while Hudson had dysentery on top of his other health problems. Wang Lae-djun also became terribly sea-sick. They were all very glad when the coastline of England came into view.

The *Jubilee* docked in Gravesend in late November 1860, and they caught a train to London. In London they made their way to Bayswater and the home of Amelia and her new husband Benjamin Broomhall. Louisa, his youngest sister, now twenty years old, was also waiting for him there. They had a joyful, long-anticipated reunion, and after several days with Amelia and Benjamin, they took the train to Barnsley and a warm reunion with his parents. Before he left London, though, Amelia managed to persuade Hudson to cut off his queue and begin wearing English clothes again.

Two weeks later, Amelia and Benjamin, as well as Aunt Hannah and Uncle Richard from Hull, arrived in Barnsley for Christmas. Maria felt welcomed into Hudson's family, and just seeing everybody again made Hudson feel better.

After Christmas they returned to London and rented a house close to London Hospital. Wang Lae-djun moved in with them.

Hudson went to the hospital, where his former instructor told him that his liver, digestive system, and nervous system had all been badly damaged by his illness. Recuperation would be a long process, and it would be many years before his health was strong enough for him to travel overseas again. Despite the bad news, Hudson did not get depressed; there was too much to do.

Although he may have left China, China had not left him. The country was continually on his mind. He bought a huge map of China and pinned it to the wall opposite the desk in his study. It was the first thing he saw when he began work in the morning and the last thing he prayed for at night. Slowly, as he regained his strength, he began to plan for his eventual return to China, even though he had no idea when that would be.

Hudson's experiences with the hospital in Ning-po had shown him the need to complete his medical training. That was why he had rented a house close to London Hospital's new medical college building. Even though he started out as an outpatient at the hospital, as soon as he was strong enough, he resumed his medical studies there.

While he studied at the hospital, he started on another project. This project was the reason Wang Lae-djun had accompanied them back to England. With his help, and that of Frederick Gough, another missionary to China, they began the task of translating the New Testament in the Ning-po dialect from pictographs to romanized words. (This meant that instead of using pictures to represent Chinese words in the traditional way, the sounds of the words themselves were written out phonetically using letters of the alphabet.) Translating the New Testament this way would make it much easier for Chinese people and missionaries alike to learn how to read Chinese.

Hudson also began recruiting workers to go to Ning-po and help John Jones run the Bridge Street Chapel, as the church there was now called.

All of this kept Hudson very busy. In fact, it took four years to complete it all. By 1865, the New Testament had been translated and Wang Lae-djun had returned to his family in Ning-po with the completed text. Six new workers had also been sent to Ning-po. Dr. Parker himself, having remarried, returned to restart the hospital. And Hudson had his medical degree. He was a member of the Royal College of Surgeons and had the title "Doctor" in front of his name.

During this time, Hudson received no wages for his efforts, so he and Maria relied on God to meet their needs. Sometimes God's provision arrived at the last moment, but always, even when their three new sons, Herbert, then Howard, and finally little Samuel, were born, there was enough money for the rent and food.

As the days went by and Hudson studied the large map on his wall, an idea began to grow in his mind. China had eleven provinces and one territory, Mongolia. Hudson prayed for them every day. *How hard would it be to recruit two missionaries to go into each of those areas? By year's end, every province in China could have its own missionaries sharing the Gospel with the people there.* The idea excited him. It would take only twenty-four missionaries to do it. It could easily be done if the mission societies with missionaries already in China agreed to take part in the plan. So Hudson began visiting the local representatives of these societies to get them to help.

The representatives he visited were polite but firm. They all gave the same answer. They didn't have enough money or the right personnel to send missionaries into the interior. It was hard enough to support the missionaries already in China. In fact, the year before there had been a total of one hundred fifteen Protestant missionaries in China. This year the number was down to ninety-one. Hudson, they pointed out, needed to accept the reality that China was no longer a fashionable place to send missionaries; it was dangerous and very foreign.

Hudson could hardly believe what he was hearing. With that kind of attitude, there would be no missionaries left in China in a few years, and just at the time when the country was really beginning to open up. They had to keep sending missionaries! Every month more than a million Chinese people died without ever hearing about Jesus Christ.

Over and over Hudson asked himself the question, *Why wasn't someone doing something?* As he thought about it, the question slowly and quietly turned itself around in his mind: *Why aren't I doing something?*

Deep in his heart he struggled with the answer. He knew there was no one in England better suited to recruit a group of missionaries to move into the heart of China than he and Maria, but he did not want the responsibility for other people's lives. It was too great a load to bear, having others rely on him for their safety and guidance. On his return to China, Dr. Parker had fallen off a horse into an icy river and drowned. One of the six missionaries Hudson had recruited and sent to Ning-po had contracted cholera and died. Even his good friend, John Jones, had become so sick that he had to return to England. On the voyage home he'd died, and now lay buried on some faraway, forgotten island. Such sad news made Hudson long to be in China to help and encourage those left working there, but how could he accept the responsibility for the lives of others who might go?

He felt caught in the middle. Part of him wanted to organize an all-out missionary assault on China, but another part of him was too scared to ask people to go, knowing he would be responsible for them.

Hudson became very stressed over the whole matter. He couldn't seem to sleep or eat, and his health was starting to deteriorate again.

Maria could see the strain in her husband, and she was pleased when he announced he was going to Brighton for a few days' rest. He would stay with Mr. Berger, the man who had begun supporting the hospital work in Ning-po right at the time they ran out of money. Maria hoped the sea air and the Christian fellowship would help clear Hudson's mind.

Unfortunately, the large church filled with happy, healthy, rich Christians had the opposite effect on Hudson. He found it hard to sit and listen to people singing about God and their salvation while not seeming to care whether others went to their eternal death without ever hearing the Gospel.

Hudson could no longer stand to be in the service. He slipped out a side door and, as the organ music faded behind him, walked down to Brighton Beach. He took off his shoes and socks and waded in the water. His heart was as tossed and turned as the seaweed floating in the surf. He had to resolve the struggle he felt inside. As the waves lapped around his feet, a thought suddenly occurred to him. *What was the worst thing that could happen to a missionary in his care? What if he took a group of missionaries back to China and they all died? How bad would that be in the light of eternity? They would all go straight to heaven. And if, as a result of their work and sacrifice, one Chinese person turned to Christ, wouldn't that make it worthwhile?*

Strangely, this backward way of looking at things comforted Hudson. *In the light of eternity*, there was no fate worse than for Chinese people never to hear the Gospel.

As he thought about all this, his mind began to clear. If each missionary was obeying God in going to China, the responsibility for what happened to them rested with God, and not with Hudson Taylor. Tears of joy slid down his cheeks. The answer to his struggle was so simple. He was going to do what he felt God was calling him to do, and he would trust that others exercised the same obedience. Standing in ankle-deep water on Brighton Beach, Hudson prayed and asked God to raise up twenty-four workers for China. Then he pulled a pencil from his pocket and wrote in the back of his Bible, "Prayed for twenty-four willing, skillful laborers at Brighton, June 25, 1865."

The next day, he returned to London a new man. The inner conflict was settled; it was time to move forward. Now he had to prepare for what God wanted him to do.

He went to the London and County Bank and, with ten pounds, opened a bank account in the name of the *China Inland Mission*.

Next, Hudson took all the information he'd gathered together to try to convince existing missionary societies to join his plan, and he put it into a booklet. He called the booklet *China's Spiritual Need and Claims*.

The booklet set out plainly how four hundred million Chinese people had never heard the Gospel. Yet they had a right to hear it, and Christians in other lands around the world had a duty to follow Jesus' command to go into all the world and preach the Gospel.

The booklet made many Christians feel uncomfortable. Was it possible that they were partly responsible for the million people in China who died each month without knowing of Jesus Christ?

Even though it made people feel uncomfortable, *China's Spiritual Need and Claims* was a best-seller. It was reprinted time and again, as more and more people read it and shared it with their friends.

It was as if God had been waiting for Hudson to make a commitment before unleashing His blessing. In what was at first a dribble, and then a flood, money, supplies, and workers began to pour in.

Some readers were so inspired by what Hudson had written that they wrote and told him his vision wasn't big enough. A wealthy friend, Lord Radstock, wrote, "I read your pamphlet on the way down here and have been greatly stirred by it....Dear brother, enlarge your desires. Ask for a hundred laborers and the Lord will give them to you!" Enclosed with the letter was a check for a hundred pounds.

As workers and money flooded in, people began asking Hudson how the new mission would work and what its rules were. They were good questions, but Hudson didn't have the answers to them. So he gathered together a group of trusted friends and church leaders to pray and ask God to show them how the mission should work. Over several days of meetings, six principles emerged that they all agreed the new mission should be based upon. These principles were: (1) the workers could be from any Christian denomination as long as they agreed to work together; (2) the missionaries would not receive a salary from China Inland Mission (CIM), but together they would trust God to supply all their needs; (3) the CIM would never ask for money from anyone except God; (4) the mission leaders in China would be free to make decisions about what to do next and would not have to wait for orders from England; (5) the workers would be part of an organized plan to evangelize the whole of China; (6) CIM missionaries would live as much like Chinese people as they possibly could. They would wear Chinese clothes, eat with chopsticks, and live in Chinese-style homes.

The years of quiet recuperation, study, and translation were over for the Taylors. There were so many things to organize and supervise. By May 1866, Hudson had spoken at meetings and rallies from one end of England to the other, as well as in Scotland and Ireland. Many people had offered prayer, money, or themselves to reach the people of China with the Gospel.

Time was drawing near for the Taylors, their four children, and the first group of sixteen missionaries to leave for China. When they arrived in China, they would be joined by the missionaries Hudson had recruited earlier and sent to Ning-po. All the group needed now was several hundred pounds to pay for their passage and a ship with enough space to transport them all. Hudson had seen God work in many wonderful ways during the past four years in London. He had no doubt God would quickly meet their remaining needs.

While the team waited in London to see how God would get them to China, Hudson accepted an invitation to speak at a large gathering at a place called Totteridge. The gathering was like so many others Hudson had spoken at in the past few months. It was organized by John Puget, a retired Army colonel. During the service, Hudson held up a map of China and told those in attendance about his plan to reach the whole interior of the country with the Gospel. He used Scotland as an example. In Scotland, there were several thousand ministers to care for Scottish Christians, and everyone had access to Bibles and Christian books. In China, it was the exact opposite. There was not even one minister for every four thousand people in China. Surely, Hudson pointed out, it was the duty of Christians in Scotland and every other Christian nation to reach out to China.

After he finished speaking, Hudson dismissed the meeting and sat down. Nobody moved; the room was silent. People had never heard the challenge to take the Gospel to every person put quite the way Hudson had put it.

Colonel Puget, who was a quick thinker, saw a wonderful opportunity. The new mission surely needed money, and many people in the audience would be glad to give it. The colonel jumped to his feet. "Brothers and sisters in Christ," he began, "tonight we have heard from a remarkable man with a remarkable vision. The flyer advertising this meeting said there would be no money collected, but I know many of you would be upset if you could not give. I am sure Dr. Taylor would not mind if we took a collection."

Now it was Hudson's turn to jump to his feet. "Mr. Chairman, I beg you to keep to the conditions we agreed to," he said. "If after thought and prayer the congregation is satisfied that a gift of money is what God wants them to give, then it can be given to any missionary society with missionaries in China, or it can be mailed to our London office."

Later that night at Colonel Puget's house, where Hudson was staying, the colonel challenged Hudson about his views. "Why not let people give to God's work if they want to?" he asked.

Hudson explained that often money is the easiest thing to give. "I think a collection tends to leave the impression that the all-important thing is money, whereas no amount of money can convert a single soul. What is needed is men and women filled with the Holy Spirit to give themselves to the work. There will never be a shortage of funds for the support of such people," he said.

Colonel Puget shook his head, "I think you are mistaken. A good opportunity was lost tonight."

The two men went to bed, and the next morning Hudson was up bright and early. He was in the middle of breakfast when a letter arrived from London. It was from Maria, and he ripped it open, eager to read how things were going. As he read it, he smiled. A ship big enough for them all had just docked. It was called the *Lammermuir*, and it was looking for passengers for its next trip to Shanghai leaving May 26.

Hudson was still thinking of all he had to do, including praying about the remaining money they needed for the trip to Shanghai, when Colonel Puget came in. The colonel looked tired and ate his breakfast in near silence.

When he'd finished eating, he asked Hudson to follow him into his study. He cleared his throat and began speaking. "Last night, I was convinced you were wrong about the collection. Now I'm convinced you were right. As I thought about what you said in the meeting and the ceaseless flow of people headed to a Christless eternity, I could only pray as you suggested, 'Lord, what would you have me do?' I think I obtained the guidance I sought, and here it is."

Colonel Puget handed Hudson a check for five hundred pounds.

"If there had been a collection last night, I would have put in only a five-pound note," he added.

Hudson thanked Colonel Puget for his hospitality and for the money and hurried back to London. He knew just what to do with the money when he got there. He met with Captain Bell and inspected the *Lammermuir*. The ship was perfect for their plans. She was two years old, a square-rigger with a steel frame and three masts. And Captain Bell assured Hudson she could withstand the fiercest storm.

Hudson handed Colonel Puget's check to Captain Bell as down payment on their passage.

The captain, a new Christian, was delighted at the prospect of having a band of missionaries aboard his ship, though he warned Hudson that the crew were a rough bunch.

Hudson hurried back to the house to tell the rest of the group that they were officially on their way to China.

Chapter 13

"Were We Never to Reach China"

It was May 25, 1866. The following day, the first official group of missionaries from the China Inland Mission would set sail aboard the *Lammermuir*, bound for Shanghai. Hudson put his pen down and smiled. He had just completed writing a passenger list to give to Captain Bell the next day.

He looked at the list. His name was at the top, along with Maria's and their four children, six-year-old Grace, five-year-old Herbert, three-year-old Howard, and little Samuel, nearly two years old. He hoped Samuel wouldn't be cutting any teeth while they were at sea. He still had vivid memories of the journey home, sitting through the night with the teething Grace.

Listed below the children were the names of the only other married couple in the group, Lewis and Eliza Nicol. Lewis was a blacksmith from Scotland. Below them were the names of five single men: James Williamson, George Duncan, Josiah Jackson, John Sell, and William Rudland. Following them were the names of the single women: Jane McLean, Emily Blatchley, Jennie Faulding, Mary Bausum, Mary Bell, Louise Desgraz, Elizabeth Rose, Mary Bowyer, and Susan Barnes.

Hudson prayed for each name on the list and asked God to give each person strength for the journey. He thought about each one. He remembered how they had come to him with their eyes shining and their faith strong. He'd told each one plainly about the potential dangers that lay ahead, and each one had looked him straight in the eye and told him he was called by God to take the Gospel to Inland China, whatever the cost.

The men and women made a good team. Most of them were not scholars. They were secretaries, stonemasons, carpenters, and teachers, but they had an enthusiasm to share God's love with people. Any other skill or knowledge they needed, Hudson was sure they could learn later. Most importantly, they had a love for God and a praying heart, and that was the core of a missionary with the China Inland Mission.

Hudson also prayed for their departure. He knew how difficult it was to say goodbye, especially for the parents and family staying behind. There was a cost to count, and some of those saying goodbye tomorrow would never see each other again this side of heaven. And while he would do everything he could to make sure those in his party were safe, both on the voyage and when they got to China, each one felt he was called to go, so the real responsibility for his safety and well-being rested with God.

When he'd finished praying, Hudson went downstairs. The house was in an uproar. There were people and baggage and noise filling every room. The children were running in and out among the sea chests. Jennie Faulding was showing her parents the map of China and pointing out where they would be staying at first and where they hoped to eventually go. George Duncan and James Williamson were unscrewing the legs from the harmonium and packing it into a crate. It would be one of the first things to be unpacked once they were aboard the *Lammermuir*.

The farewell the next day went smoothly. Of course, there were many tears as people embraced friends and family. Amelia and Benjamin, Louisa, and Mrs. Taylor were all there to say goodbye. Mr. Berger and his wife also came to wish them well. As the *Lammermuir* prepared to leave the East India Company dock in London, those standing on the dock sang a hymn for those departing, and then those departing sang a hymn back in reply, as Maria accompanied them on the harmonium.

A steam tug maneuvered the *Lammermuir* out into the main channel of the river Thames. They all sang louder as the ship moved away from the dock.

On board, the *Lammermuir*'s thirty-four-man crew was worried. All their passengers were missionaries. And for the next four months, they would all be stuck together in the middle of the ocean. And, probably, every day they would have to listen to hymn singing, like the kind they had just witnessed. A long voyage always got boring, and a lively group of passengers could help pass the time quickly. But eighteen Bible-carrying, hymn-singing missionaries and four children were not exactly what they had in mind.

Several crew members were complaining to Captain Bell about their passengers before the *Lammermuir* had even reached Gravesend at the mouth of the river Thames. The captain just smiled as he listened to their grumbling. He, for one, was looking forward to spending time with Hudson and his group.

The whole group stayed on deck until the coastline of England had faded from view. Maria and Emily Blatchley busily tried to supervise the children. Hudson could see that the boys were going to be a handful; the ship was small, and the boys needed to keep out of the way of the crew. There were also many dangerous things on board they could get caught in, such as pulleys and winches and ropes and chains, not to mention the danger of falling overboard.

As the *Lammermuir* headed for the English Channel, Hudson stood on the poop deck and committed the voyage to God. He was grateful that

across the British Isles pockets of people were praying for them. It was true, many Christians had criti-
cized the China Inland Mission and its ideas of
trusting God alone, but as long as there were people
committed to pray for them, Hudson was confident
all would be well. When people questioned how he
could lead a group that included nine single
women into the heart of a heathen country without
financial support, his answer was always the same:
"I am taking my children with me, and I notice it's
not difficult for me to remember that they need
breakfast in the morning, lunch at midday, and dinner before they go to bed. I find it impossible to
believe our Heavenly Father is less tender or mind-
ful than I am."

"Excuse me, Dr. Taylor, but where should I put
the spare rollers for the press? The hold is full." It
was James Williamson, and his question brought
Hudson back to the present. There were still things
that needed to be stowed away for the voyage.
England was gone from view now; it was time to
focus on matters at hand.

By Tuesday, everything was in order, and life
settled into a routine. Hudson taught a Chinese language class every morning, and for a change of
voice, Maria taught the class in the afternoon.

There was plenty of time in the late afternoon and
early evening for other things. Everyone wrote letters, hoping a ship headed for England might come
alongside and take them back. Otherwise, the letters
would be mailed when they reached Shanghai.

Captain Bell had been right about the crew. They were rough and loud. The children had to be instructed to ignore their cursing. But as tough as the crew seemed, for the next four months, they were to be the mission field of the fledgling China Inland Mission.

Mary Bell began holding a nightly Bible study, and to her surprise, many of the sailors attended it. They came not so much because they were interested in what she had to say, but because she was pretty.

Louise Desgraz held Bible readings in Swedish for the four crew members from Sweden. Susan Barnes held classes for those who wanted to improve their reading, and a number of the crew began attending.

Hudson was delighted that he didn't have to remind anyone in the group of his or her obligation to reach out to the crew with the Gospel message. Before they left England, he'd stressed to them that "a voyage across the ocean will not make anyone a soul winner." By this he meant that a desire to share God's love with everyone had to be in their hearts wherever they found themselves. Simply being given the title of missionary would not magically make them missionaries.

The group also found practical ways to help around the ship. As on the *Dumfries*, Hudson served as the ship's doctor. He gave lectures on first aid, the circulation of the blood, and the construction of the eye, subjects that sailors would not have found very exciting on land, but in the middle of the ocean they drew quite a crowd.

Lewis Nicol forged parts for the crane hooks, while James Williamson and William Rudland tinkered with the bilge pumps until they worked perfectly. Slowly but surely, the missionaries began to win the begrudging respect of the crew.

The crew no longer complained about the hymn singing. In fact, they had heard some of the hymns so many times that they found themselves singing along without even realizing it! Then one or two of the crew began to have things to do around the ship's saloon when the group were holding their meetings. They would splice rope or check a deck joint nearby. After a couple of weeks, they did not bother with excuses; they just pulled up a barrel outside the saloon and sat down and listened.

First one, then two, three, four, and more crewmen asked Jesus Christ into their lives and became Christians. Before the voyage was even half over, twenty-three crew members had become Christians. The young missionaries eagerly discipled the new converts. The crew asked Hudson to move his daily meeting out on deck because the saloon was becoming too cramped.

But the more the crew found peace with God, the less peace they found with the first mate, Mr. Brunton. He was second in command aboard the *Lammermuir*, and he didn't like what was happening with his crew. Mr. Brunton had a bad temper, which, unfortunately for all on board, seemed to be touched off by any mention of religion. As time went by, he became increasingly angry and began bullying many of the new converts on his crew. Mr. Brunton soon became the focus of prayer for many people on board, both passengers and crew. And slowly, he began to soften. He began to allow Hudson to read passages from the Bible to him and explain their meaning. One night in August, Hudson read him the Passover story from the book of Exodus. When he came to the passage where God tells the Israelites to paint blood on the door posts so death would pass over their houses, Mr. Brunton jumped to his feet yelling, "'When I see the blood it will pass over you.' I see. I see. How blind I've been."

Hudson was so excited he woke up John Sell and Elizabeth Rose, who had been praying hard for Mr. Brunton, and told them the good news of his conversion. John Sell looked at his pocket watch; it was three-thirty in the morning.

The next day, Mr. Brunton called the entire crew together and apologized to them for the way he'd been behaving. An amazing change took place in his life. From then on, he was at every meeting, singing as loud as he could, and he was usually the last to leave.

Hudson was excited at the influence his group was having on the crew. He wrote a letter to Mr. Berger and said, "Our minds are kept in peace as to the future. Were we never to reach China, we should all rejoice in the work God has done on the *Lammermuir.*"

When Hudson wrote the words, "Were we never to reach China," he had no idea of the test that lay ahead for them all.

It was September 10; six more days and they would be in Shanghai. The crew was busy scrubbing the decks and painting the bulwarks (the railing and side of the ship above the deck), and preparing for their arrival. Hudson had rigged up a system so that the missionaries could pull buckets of sea water in through the port holes in their cabins and take a bath in a tin bathtub. They were each taking turns at having a bath, and Susan Barnes was giving everyone a haircut so they would look well-groomed on arrival. Emily Blatchley and Maria were busy patching the holes the young Taylor boys had worn in their pants crawling around the *Lammermuir.* Everyone was looking forward to their first glimpse of China.

But things weren't right. The weather was beginning to get squally, and the barometric pressure was falling. Captain Bell didn't say much about it at first. He hoped they were only heading into a light storm. Unfortunately, it wasn't to be. The *Lammermuir* was directly in the path of a typhoon.

Captain Bell finally ordered everything on deck to be lashed down with ropes and the sails to be pulled down and stowed so they wouldn't be torn to shreds by the wind. Having been through the nightmare of the storm on the *Dumfries,* Hudson calmed the fears of those in his party and helped them tie themselves into their bunks.

For two nights, the *Lammermuir* was tossed about mercilessly by the sea. Huge waves rolled across the decks and spilled water into the saloon. Then, as quickly as it had come, the storm left. Everyone came up on deck to survey the damage. From the look of things, it was just as well the storm had ended when it did: the *Lammermuir* couldn't have stood much more of the sea's pounding. The lifeboats had been washed away, and so had the pens where the animals were kept, along with the last few remaining animals. The ship was in need of repairs, but with calm seas and better weather, she would easily make it to her destination.

The next three days were spent drying out the sails, pumping the bilge, and tightening the rigging. Several barrels of food supplies had been soaked with saltwater and rain and were useless, so meals were meager. But being only a few days from Shanghai, no one was too worried. There would be plenty to eat when they reached the city.

Hudson was also glad they would be in Shanghai soon, but for another reason. Captain Bell had become ill. Hudson wasn't quite sure what the problem was, but the left half of the captain's face was paralyzed. An exact diagnosis of the problem required more medical equipment than was on board the *Lammermuir*. The sooner they got to Shanghai, the better.

That night, the barometric pressure began to drop again, and faster than it had before the previous storm. The crew and passengers held an urgent prayer meeting. If this storm was going to be worse than the last one, only God could get them through it. The battered *Lammermuir* was in no condition to battle her way through another storm.

By the time they had finished praying, the wind was howling across the decks, snatching up barrels of supplies as though they weighed nothing and hurling them into the ocean. One minute the ship was pointed towards the sky, and the next it was skidding down the face of a mountainous wave. Hour after hour the *Lammermuir* was slammed by enormous seas.

Every time someone from the crew appeared in the saloon, he had worse news than before. The bulwarks had been washed away. Now there was nothing to stop the waves, and soon they began washing across the deck and pounded against the saloon door.

Everyone longed for the storm to end. Passengers and crew were both at exhaustion level. But the storm just continued to gather strength.

After two days of battling the storm with no food and no sleep, the crew were losing hope. Captain Bell and Mr. Brunton could no longer motivate them to work. With the bulwarks gone, there was nothing to hold on to or protect them on deck, and any or all of them could be swept overboard in an instant. Even when the jib and fore staysails, the long pieces of wood that supported the bottoms of the sails, broke loose, the crew would not go out on deck to secure them.

The jib and fore staysails swung about danger-ously in the wind. At any moment they could come crashing down. And if they did, they would go right through the deck, and the ship would surely sink.

As Captain Bell looked across the deck of his ship, his heart sank. It was the beginning of the end. The *Lammermuir* would not hold up to the pound-ing she was taking much longer. The hull seemed to creak louder with each passing hour. Still, sick as he was, he had to try to save his ship. Since the crew would not obey him, he and Mr. Brunton would have to do it alone. Together they climbed out onto the deck, hoping to grab the jib and fore staysails and tie them down. They crawled along, low to the deck, so the swinging jib would not knock them overboard. Just as they were getting ready to grab the jib, a massive wave struck the ship. The two men clung to the main mast with all their strength to avoid being washed away. Then came the crack-ing sound they did not want to hear. Above their heads, the mast they were clinging to snapped, and so did the mizzen mast. As the two masts fell, they tangled in the rigging, which stopped them from crashing right through the deck. As carefully as they could, Captain Bell and Mr. Brunton crawled to the saloon.

With two of her three masts broken and lying across the deck, the *Lammermuir* was beginning to break up. The fallen masts battered back and forth against the deck and the side of the ship, shattering whatever wood they hit into match-sized pieces.

"It is only a matter of time now, and not much at that. If only I could get the crew to help me, we might be able to cut the rigging away and let the masts go over the side, but it's a long shot," Captain Bell told Hudson, with panic in his voice.

Hudson and Maria kissed each one of their children goodbye and commended them to God. There were no lifeboats, and even if there were, they would be useless in these violent swells. The missionaries gathered close together in the middle of the saloon and began to sing "Rock of Ages."

They were midway through the third verse of the hymn when Hudson noticed Captain Bell slip a pistol into his belt. Hudson crawled after him as he made his way across the deck. He caught up to him just as he neared the forecastle, where the crew had taken refuge. When they saw the captain with his revolver, they squashed themselves together further in the tiny space. They would rather be shot than forced out of their refuge.

"Let me talk to them," Hudson yelled over the roar of the sea.

Captain Bell nodded, and Hudson crawled into the forecastle. He raised his voice above the fury of the storm. "Men, the only hope is for us to get the masts overboard. We will help you; our lives are in as much danger as yours. Get out and help us save the ship."

The men did not move. They were as paralyzed by fear as the left side of Captain Bell's face.

Hudson gestured for Captain Bell to leave his gun in his belt, and then he crawled back to the saloon and explained the situation to the missionary men. Together they committed themselves to God and one by one crawled out of the saloon, keeping their heads down against the wind.

The missionaries fanned out across the deck, holding onto the metal rings embedded in the deck that were used for lashing down cargo. With one hand on a ring, they began to hack away at the rigging. Each man worked alone. First they freed the main mast and jettisoned it over the side; then they moved towards the stern of the ship and set to work on the mizzen mast.

Seeing the men of the China Inland Mission risking their lives to save the *Lammermuir*, members of the crew began to regain their courage. They crawled out from the forecastle and joined in the effort to save the ship.

Finally the mizzen mast fell free and was washed over the side of the ship, and the men made their way back to the saloon.

While on deck, they'd been unable see each other because of the spray and water that deluged the ship. They did not know whether anyone had been washed overboard, and they waited anxiously to see who returned. One by one the missionary men and the crew made their way into the saloon. Miraculously, not one person had been swept overboard. But the storm was not yet over, and after a quick prayer of thanks, every man and woman aboard took his or her turn manning the bilge pumps. The men and women pumped all night to keep the water that washed in through the holes in the battered deck from sinking the ship. As morning approached, the winds began to die down. By the time the sun rose, the angry sea that had almost claimed the *Lammermuir* was calm.

Five days later, broken and maimed, the *Lammermuir* limped up the Hwang-poo River into Shanghai. Curious onlookers crowded onto junks to see the ship. When they saw how damaged she was, they were amazed she'd made it to port. The crew and passengers told the story of how they had come so close to death, only to be saved when everything seemed hopeless. Other sailors shook their heads when they heard no lives had been lost and no one had been badly injured during the storms. Another ship, which had traveled the same course as the *Lammermuir*, arrived in port the following day. Its shredded flag flew at half staff. Out of a crew of twenty-two, only six had survived the storms. The other sixteen crew members either had been washed overboard or were buried at sea after being killed in horrific accidents during the storms.

After the *Lammermuir* docked, Captain Bell allowed his passengers to stay on board for a few days until they could make arrangements for somewhere to live. There had never been enough hotels in Shanghai, and Hudson knew that none of the other missionaries in the city would have enough rooms for eighteen adults and four children to stay in, not to mention space to store their printing presses and hospital equipment.

The following day, the members of the China Inland Mission, newly arrived in China, prayed hard that God would provide a solution to their need for accommodation. Against all odds, God had brought them this far unharmed. They knew He would not let them down now. Somewhere there was a place for them to stay, and God would lead them to it.

Chapter 14

The Work Begins

The new missionaries of the China Inland Mission did not have to wait long for God to answer their prayers for accommodation. The first missionary to come aboard the *Lammermuir* to welcome them to China was William Gamble, of the American Presbyterian Mission. William Gamble had been living in Ning-po at the same time as Hudson, and they had become friends. Now he was excited to be welcoming his old friend back to China.

William Gamble was the printer for the American Presbyterian Mission, and he had recently moved from Ning-po to Shanghai to set up a new printing press. He had bought a large warehouse close to the old city to house the new press, but the printing equipment had been delayed. So his warehouse stood empty. When he found out the new missionaries had nowhere to stay, he insisted they use his warehouse for as long as they liked while they arranged the permits they needed to move inland. The warehouse would be more than big enough for all of them and their equipment and supplies. The next day, the group joyfully unloaded their belongings from the *Lammermuir* and moved into the warehouse.

After drying out their wet belongings and washing all of their clothes and bedding, it was time for them to get down to business. Hudson hired a barber, who shaved the front of each man's head and wove a false queue into the hair that was left. Next the group were all outfitted with Chinese clothes. As they emerged from the warehouse onto the street, a collection of both foreigners and Chinese stopped to look and laugh. The men, in particular, had a difficult time keeping their pants pulled up and not tripping over the curled-up ends of their new shoes. There was even an article in the Shanghai newspaper about the new China Inland Mission. In the article, the writer called them the "Pigtail Mission."

To many foreigners in Shanghai, the behavior of the new mission was both un-British and un-Christian. Missionaries from other organizations often crossed the street when they saw someone from the China Inland Mission approaching. They wanted nothing to do with such a weird group of people.

All of this caused some of the new missionaries to wonder whether wearing Chinese clothing and having a Chinese hairstyle was the right approach. But Hudson reminded them they would be leaving soon for the interior, where they would meet multiplied thousands of people who had never seen a white person before. "Do you want to be remembered for the strange Western clothes you wore, or for the message of salvation you preached?" he asked them. The new missionaries could see his point and spent more time practicing how to roll up the sleeves of their tunics and eat rice with chopsticks.

Three weeks after arriving, the paperwork was complete, and the China Inland Mission had permission to leave Shanghai for Hang-chow. Before they left, several missionaries from other groups came to talk to Hudson. They told him he was crazy. How could he encourage nine unmarried women to venture into the interior? Didn't he know that in all of China, there was not one unmarried woman working away from the five treatyports?

Hudson did know, and as they spoke he thought back to Brighton Beach and all God had shown him there. He would do all he could to keep the women safe, but God had called them, and each woman knew the risks involved.

William Gamble had grown attached to the missionaries staying in his warehouse. He was sad to see them go, and he did not want to take the rent money they insisted on paying him. He came to the dock to see them off. It was a beautiful, moonlit night when they boarded the junks that would take them a hundred miles up the Hwang-poo River to Hang-chow. William Gamble helped them aboard, and before waving goodbye, he left a small package on the seat of the last junk. When the package was opened, it contained all the rent money they had paid him for use of the warehouse and a note that read, "For the good of the mission."

The junks floated silently out onto the river, past the docks, where the *Lammermuir* was still tied up undergoing repairs. The crew had been looking out for the missionaries, and when they saw them, they begged Hudson to come aboard for one last service. By the light of the moon, the missionaries clambered up the rope ladder over the side of the ship onto the familiar deck of the *Lammermuir*. Hudson preached a short sermon on the foredeck, and they sang some hymns together. Mr. Brunton asked if he could travel upstream with the party for a few days, and Captain Bell gave his permission. So with one more member than when they had started, the group reboarded their junks. As they floated out on the river, the crew and the missionaries sang together "Yes We Part, But Not Forever," the same hymn that had annoyed so many of the crew when they first heard it on the East India Company dock in London. Now they themselves were singing it as loud as they could, not caring what the sailors on nearby ships thought.

Mr. Brunton traveled with them for three days, and Hudson baptized him in the river before he returned to the *Lammermuir* in Shanghai.

The trip to Hang-chow was very slow, and it was four weeks before the junks finally docked there. The city of a million people was as beautiful as Hudson had told everyone it would be. Although heavily damaged during the Taiping Rebellion, it had been mostly rebuilt, and there were lots of lakes and open fields in and around the city.

Just as in Shanghai, there were few houses to rent in Hang-chow, but after several days, Hudson managed to find the perfect place, that is, if you used a lot of imagination. The house at number One New Lane was one of those buildings that had not been repaired after the Taiping Rebellion. It had enormous holes in its walls, and what was left of the walls was caked with mud. But the house was also huge. It was a two-storied building and had over thirty rooms. Hudson could immediately see the possibilities. There would be a hospital and dispensary downstairs and living space upstairs. The house also had a courtyard with a beautiful rock garden and pond where the children could play safely.

The team set about quietly repairing the house. They knew most of the people in the city had never seen a foreigner before, and they didn't want to scare them. So they left the windows open and curtains undrawn most of the time so their neighbors could see what they were doing. Soon they had little groups of Chinese people watching them eat rice and vegetables with chopsticks and swat the flies away with large grass fans.

Slowly, the people peering in through the windows got braver. They hung around the doorway and finally ventured inside. One or two curious people opened up a sea chest to see what was kept inside. They turned the handle on the clothes wringer and pretended to feed clothes through it like the foreign women did. A few of the braver ones examined the women's long hair, which came in strange colors: white like a silk worm's thread or brown like hemp rope. They looked into the foreigners' blue and gray eyes, and they laughed at their long, bumpy noses. They rubbed freckles to see if they were painted on, and came to the conclusion that although the foreigners had some unfortunate deformities, they were not all that different from themselves.

News of the friendly foreigners spread through the city. Before long the house on New Lane was a hive of activity. The hospital opened, and soon over two hundred patients a day were coming to receive medical care. Tsui, one of the converts from the Bridge Street church in Ning-po, joined the team. He spent his days preaching and talking to the crowds that came to the house. After particularly difficult operations, to remove cataracts, for example, Hudson would take a break by singing hymns and playing the harmonium. The patients loved it. Hudson would sing at the top of his voice and then climb on top of a desk and preach his heart out. Life was never dull at the house on New Lane.

Maria often sat with the patients, praying with those who seemed frightened and telling Bible stories to the children. She also had another baby of her own to look after. Little Maria was the baby sister Grace had wanted for so long.

In late summer, the Taylor family took a much-needed break. Maria and the five children, Grace, Herbert, Howard, Samuel, and little Maria, stayed in the mountains outside the city while Hudson divided his time between there and the work in Hang-chow.

The children found new energy to climb and explore away from the heat of the city. They ran and swam all day long, wearing themselves out by nightfall. But one morning, about a week into their stay in the mountains, Grace did not want to get out of bed. Maria brought her food, but Grace was not hungry. As the day wore on, Maria became very concerned, so she sent for Hudson. By the time he arrived, Grace's temperature was soaring. He examined her carefully. Then he quietly slipped out of the room and motioned for Maria to follow him. He walked silently down to the pond where the children liked to swim. Then he spoke to Maria in a halting voice. "There is no hope of Grace getting better. She has meningitis, and there is no cure."

Someone stayed with Grace every minute, wiping her brow, singing to her, and praying for her. Five days later, while Hudson and Maria and many of those who had been with them on the *Lammermuir* gathered around her bed and sang hymns, Grace died peacefully.

Hudson missed her terribly; he cried for days. Everything he did and saw reminded him of Grace. He walked past the lake and saw the swans they liked to feed together. He looked out his surgery window and saw the little swing in the courtyard that she had asked him to make for her. It now hung still.

But the work in Hang-chow went on. And while there was sorrow, there was also joy. William Rudland and Mary Bell were married. Wang Lae-djun, who had accompanied Hudson and Maria to England seven years before, joined them. "Pastor" Wang, as he was now called, started a small church. Soon it had fifty baptized believers. The church was active in reaching out to the rest of the community with the Gospel message. Four other mission stations were also opened in nearby cities, and the China Inland Mission was beginning to grow as new missionaries arrived from England.

There were still so many other challenges in China, though, and Hudson was getting restless. He had been in Hang-chow for nearly two years, and it was time for him to move farther inland. Jennie Faulding and the McCarthys, who had joined the team in Hang-chow from England, agreed to stay and support Wang Lae-djun while the rest of the group packed their belongings once again. In June

1868, they boarded a houseboat headed for Yang-chow, two hundred miles farther inland.

They sailed up the Grand Canal, crossed the Yangtze River, and then sailed another twelve miles up the canal until they arrived in Yang-chow, the city Marco Polo had been governor of in the thirteenth century. Like Tung-chow, which Hudson had visited thirteen years before with John Burdon, Yang-chow was know for the unruly behavior of its inhabitants. Aware of this, the members of the China Inland Mission stayed quietly on their houseboat until late July, when they moved into a large house Hudson had rented.

The house was close to several other houses and had a number of outbuildings for team members to live in. Hudson hired some carpenters, who spent several weeks working to repair and improve the house so that the team would be able to make better use of it for their ministry.

Few foreigners had ventured into Yang-chow, and so the team were very cautious as they made contact with the local inhabitants. A number of the educated people in the city were not happy to see the foreign missionaries. They believed that the foreigners would undermine their Confucianist beliefs. So they began spreading rumors about the group, saying they ate babies and gouged out the eyes of dying people. The locals believed what they heard and what they read on the posters that appeared around the city, listing all the disgusting practices the foreigners engaged in. People began to gather outside the China Inland Mission house and chant and jeer at those inside. At first there had been a hundred protesters, but each night there were more. Finally, on Saturday night, August 22, 1868, there were nearly ten thousand protesters gathered outside the house.

The chanting of the mob filled the house. "The foreign devils have eaten twenty-four children. The foreign devils have eaten twenty-four children," the mob screamed. Rocks and mud balls exploded against the courtyard walls, and angry people pushed at the gate, which was chained shut.

"There must be at least eight thousand of them," Hudson said to Maria. "And every one of them thinks we want to eat their children. No wonder they're angry."

Maria nodded. Herbert, Howard, Samuel, and little Maria were huddled around their mother, who was holding her newest baby, Charles.

The missionaries quickly began barricading themselves in the house. They nailed the shutters closed and piled tables and other furniture in front of the door. Hudson then gathered them all together. In addition to Maria and himself and their five children, there were three men and five women from the China Inland Mission as well as nineteen Chinese Christians in the house. "The crowd is very angry. I don't think they'll stop until they have revenge," said Hudson.

William Rudland and Henry Reid nodded. Some of the earlier crowds had been ugly, but nothing like this.

"Our best hope," Hudson went on, "is to get to the mandarin quickly and ask him for help. He is the only one who can stop this."

"I'll go," volunteered George Duncan.

"Me too," added William Rudland.

"No," said Hudson. "The mandarin knows me. He knows I am the leader of the mission. I must go. George will come with me. William, you stay here and help Henry to protect the others."

Hudson kissed Maria and the children goodbye and, with George Duncan, slipped out into the courtyard and disappeared through a neighbor's house.

They walked quickly once they reached the street that backed onto their house. If they kept their heads down and did not run, maybe they wouldn't be recognized. But some of the mob caught sight of them, even in their Chinese dress and queues, as they rounded a corner. As the mob began to call after them, Hudson and George Duncan looked at each other, then began to run for their lives.

Fortunately it was getting dark, and Hudson knew a shortcut through some fields. After a while, the men looked behind them. No one was following.

They ran on, knowing that the crowd would guess they were headed for the mandarin's house.

If the crowd got to his gate first, they would have no hope of getting in to see him.

They rounded a corner and there was the gate to the mandarin's house about thirty feet in front of them. But racing from the other direction was the mob, knives drawn and yelling at the top of their voices. It was too late for Hudson and George Duncan to turn back. They had to get to the gate first. Faster and faster they ran, getting closer to the gate and to the mob. As the mob was about to grab them, they pushed the gate open and fell into the mandarin's courtyard. But they had to act quickly. The mandarin had to know they were in his courtyard and under his protection.

"Save life! Save life!" Hudson yelled at the top of his voice, as he regained his balance and rushed towards the house.

"Save life" were the only two words a mandarin had to respond to, and quickly the mandarin's secretary came running out to see what the commotion was. The mob drew back when they saw him. They had lost the opportunity to get their hands on the foreign devils, who were under the mandarin's protection now.

The secretary invited the two men inside and asked them to wait. The China Inland Mission house was a mile away, and as they waited, Hudson and George Duncan could hear the thousands of people yelling and chanting outside the house. It was impossible to imagine what might be happening to those inside. They prayed as hard as they could while they waited for the mandarin.

Back at the house, the women and children had been sent upstairs while the men stayed below to keep the barricades in place as long as they could. There was a rhythmic slamming against the front door until finally a hammer smashed through it and the table that was propped against it. The men looked around desperately for something to rein-force the barricade with, but there was nothing.

The barricades would be completely down in a few more seconds, and William Rudland ran for the stairs. He had to warn the women, even though there was no way out from the second floor. Henry Reid fled into the garden.

About this time, the mandarin finally agreed to see Hudson and George Duncan. After greeting each other, Hudson, fluent in the Mandarin dialect, explained that their house was under siege and that many foreign lives were in danger.

The mandarin nodded and frowned. "I wonder why?" he asked.

"Because all sorts of false rumors have been spread over Yang-chow. This morning a new poster said we ate babies," replied Hudson.

"And what do you really do with the babies you capture? Where are they now? Are you going to take any more?" asked the mandarin politely.

Hudson was shocked by his questions. Did the mandarin believe the lies as well? Hudson tried to stay calm. "We have come here to help the babies, not to hurt them. I'm sure you will not find one baby missing in the whole of Yang-chow. But it would be a pity to find that out after we are all dead."

"Yes," agreed the mandarin. "But why would the crowds be rioting if there were no reason to do so?"

Hudson bit his lip in frustration. "They have been told some incorrect things. May I suggest that first you quiet the crowd and then continue the questions." Hudson spoke as earnestly and as forthrightly as he could.

"Yes. Yes. That is a good solution to the problem. You stay here out of sight, and I will see what can be done," said the mandarin as he left the room.

Once again Hudson and George Duncan were left alone to wait. They could still hear the shouting and banging in the background.

They prayed and waited, and prayed some more. An hour went by. They began to wonder if the mandarin might not be just drinking tea in the next room waiting for the crowd to kill everyone before coming back to tell them he'd got there too late.

Another hour went by. Now, the noise of the riot had finally died down. Hudson and George Duncan wondered why. More time passed. Finally the mandarin walked back into the room. "Everything is quiet now," he said. "The city's military governor and soldiers have been to your home. They have made some arrests, mainly of people looting your property. They will be punished. You may return home now. I will send an escort to see you safely there, and I will post guards at your gate tonight."

Hudson's heart sank. If people had been looting the house, that meant the barricades had given way. If the mob had managed to get inside, what had happened to Maria and the children and the other missionaries?

When they finally reached the house, Hudson could see smoke rising from it. The two men kicked their way through the wreckage. Books were ripped apart and scattered across the floor. One wall had been burned, and sacks of rice had been split open and dumped everywhere. The furniture was smashed, but there were no people or bodies in the house. A new convert who'd been in the house came running in.

"Come here, come here," he said, gesturing for them to follow.

Hudson and George Duncan ran out after him. He led them through the courtyard and into a neighbor's home. In an inner courtyard of the house they found everyone safe. Hudson cried with relief when he saw them.

They told him their tale of escape. When the barricades had been breached, William Rudland had run upstairs to warn the women, while Henry Reid had fled into the garden. The women and William Rudland were trapped upstairs. Their only escape was to jump fifteen feet down into the courtyard below. They threw down pillows and quilts to break their fall. As each person jumped, Henry Reid hid them in the well house at the back of the garden.

Before they had all managed to jump to safety, some men had rushed upstairs. They robbed the women of their valuables, and when William Rudland refused to hand over his watch, one of the men picked up a brick to smash his head with. Maria threw her arms between the man and William Rudland, so the man had turned to strike her with the brick. "Would you hurt a defenseless woman?" she'd asked the man.

The man was surprised by the question, dropped the brick, and ran to the door. "Come up. Come up," he yelled to the mob below.

William Rudland and the remaining women used the opportunity to jump to safety. Unfortunately, the mob downstairs had set the pillows and quilts on fire. Henry Reid pulled them away, but now there was nothing to break their fall. Maria landed hard and twisted and cut her leg. Emily Blatchley fell backwards as she hit the ground and shattered her elbow.

Battered and bruised, they were all safe, and a neighbor gave them refuge in his inner courtyard.

Later that night, they all returned to the China Inland Mission house. The rooms had been looted. Drawers were emptied out, windows were smashed and the furniture was demolished. Amazingly, though, Emily Blatchley's room was untouched. More amazingly, it was the room where most of the mission records, important papers, and money were kept.

The next day, the mandarin sent out a proclamation warning the people of Yang-chow not to disturb the missionaries again. It ended with the words, "If anything like this occurs again, the offenders will be severely punished. Disobey not!" The proclamation was posted on every street corner.

A week after the riot, things were back to normal in the city. The missionaries repaired the house, and their ministry in Yang-chow continued on and became fruitful.

Chapter 15

A Man in Christ

By Christmas 1869, Hudson and Maria had made the most difficult decision of their married lives. Their four oldest children, Herbert, Howard, Samuel, and Maria were to be sent back to England to stay with their grandparents. It would be safer for them there, and they could go to a regular school. At that time it was quite normal for children to be sent home like this, but it still upset Hudson and Maria to think they wouldn't be seeing their children for a long time. They decided to keep one-year-old Charles with them because he was too young to be separated from his parents. Also, Maria was pregnant again and due to give birth in the middle of the year, so Charles would have a play-mate. Emily Blatchley would take the children back on the ship with her. She had contracted tuberculosis and needed treatment in England.

The family had much to do to prepare for the trip to Shanghai, where the children's ship would depart for England. As they prepared, Samuel was not well, but no one knew how sick he was until February, when they began the journey to Shanghai. As they traveled by boat down the Yangtze River, Samuel slipped into a coma and died. In the middle of a rain storm, Maria and Hudson buried their six-year-old son next to Grace in a small cemetery beside the river in the town of Chin-kiang.

As difficult as Samuel's death was for the family, they continued on their way to Shanghai. But saying goodbye to their three oldest children was not easy for Hudson and Maria. As the ship carrying their children moved off down the Hwang-poo River, they wondered if they would ever see the children again.

Around the time the children left for England, the China Inland Mission opened up many new mission stations in China, and nearly every one had problems with staff being ill or neighbors rioting. Hudson and Maria were kept very busy. They moved to Chin-kiang on the Yangtze River so they could travel to the various mission stations more easily.

On July 7, 1870, baby Noel was born. He was a solid little child, and he got bigger and stronger each day. But Maria did not. Hudson began to worry about her. She just lay in bed with Noel tucked in beside her. She smiled but looked ashen and frail.

After a week, Hudson knew her condition was serious. She was bleeding somewhere inside her body, and he had no way of knowing exactly where so he could stop it.

Meanwhile, baby Noel was no longer well either. He now had diarrhea, which is not such a big problem for an adult, but for a little baby like Noel, it was serious. Hudson now had a very sick wife and a very sick baby. He spent his time praying and helping to keep them cool and comfortable. But thirteen days after his birth, Noel's body gave up, and he died quietly, tucked in bed beside his sick mother.

Maria, who was too ill to attend the funeral, kissed her baby goodbye and chose the hymns for his funeral. Hudson left the cemetery after burying Noel beside his sister Grace and brother Samuel. But one week later he was back again. This time to bury his wife beside the children.

Maria's funeral was one of the largest ever in the area. Everyone wore white, the Chinese color of mourning. Hudson spoke at the service. He told about Maria's missionary parents, her call to China, and her love for God. Maria was thirty-three years old when she died.

Hudson missed Maria terribly. Nothing was quite the same without her beside him. Seven months earlier at Christmas, the whole family had been together. Now three members of the family were dead, three were in England, and two were left in China. Yet Hudson drew comfort from God and from the fact that one day they would all be together in heaven, and nothing would ever part them again.

In summer 1871, a year after Maria and Noel had died, Hudson felt it was time for him and Charles to visit England. He needed to spend time with the three older children and report back to the people in Great Britain who supported the mission. As it turned out, three other people from the *Lammermuir* party went with him back to England. James Meadows was sick and needed time away from China, so he and his wife, the former Elizabeth Rose, were returning home for a while. Jennie Faulding had been running several successful boarding schools for the mission. But it had been five years since she'd left England, and her parents wanted her to come home for a visit.

On the trip back to England, Mrs. Meadows spend most of the time in her cabin looking after Mr. Meadows. That left Hudson and Charles and Jennie with a lot of time to spend together. On the long voyage home, Hudson and Jennie fell in love, and they were married soon after reaching England.

Hudson returned to China with Jennie, and together they continued their work. They had two children together, Amy and Ernest. While in China, Hudson spent an increasing percentage of his time training Chinese missionaries to go into the interior to preach the Gospel.

Hudson's sister Amelia and her husband, Benjamin Broomhall, looked after Hudson's three older children, along with their own ten children. They also took over the administrative work of the China Inland Mission in London. They sent out *China's Millions*, the newsletter of the China Inland Mission. They also took care of missionaries home on leave and interviewed new missionaries for the mission.

Stories about missionaries from the China Inland Mission spread around the world. Many of the missionaries were daring and adventurous, just like their founder. Both men and women criss-crossed China, making maps of the areas they went through. John Stevenson and Henry Soltau became the first Westerners ever to cross China from west to east. They covered nineteen hundred miles in less than three months. Hudson's second wife, Jennie, and two other China Inland Mission women were the first Western women to go deep into inland China. They were on a mission to set up orphan-ages for children whose parents had died as the result of a massive famine that spread across China.

Missionaries from the China Inland Mission now no longer just came from the British Isles. There were missionaries from Sweden, the United States, and Australia. The mission quickly spread across China until there was a China Inland Mission work in every province.

By the late 1890s, though, there were many small, secret societies trying to change things inside

China. One of these groups was called the Boxers. They hated foreigners and were getting stronger as more people joined their cause. As the Boxers grew in strength, Hudson grew concerned for the safety of the missionaries, especially the single women.

At the end of 1898, the China Inland Mission had experienced what Hudson knew was a possibility ever since the day he prayed on Brighton Beach: the murder of one of its missionaries.

Bill Fleming, a lively Australian, had been on an evangelistic mission among the Black Miao tribe in the distant southwestern province of Kwei-chow. His friend and helper, P'an Shoushan, was himself a member of the Black Miao tribe. When other members of the tribe heard that P'an had left their religion to follow Christianity, they were angry. As Bill Fleming spoke to the crowd, they became even more angry, until they rushed forward to attack P'an. Fleming stepped in front of the mob, using his own body to shield his friend, and he was killed.

Hudson's heart sank as he heard the news of Bill Fleming's death. He wrote: "How sad the tidings! Blessed for the martyrs, but sad for us, for China, for their friends. And not only sad, but ominous! It seems to show that God is about to test us with a new kind of trial."

His words proved very true. Things were changing quickly in China, and changing for the worse.

Hudson continued to tell men and women everywhere about the needs of China. He traveled to Australia and New Zealand and on to the United

States. Huge crowds gathered to hear him. At Carnegie Hall in New York, thirty-five hundred came to hear him speak, including the President of the United States and the Governor of New York.

From New York he traveled on to Boston for another series of meetings. As he spoke in one of the meetings there, he seemed to forget where he was. Over and over he said the same sentence: "You may trust the Lord too little, but you can never trust Him too much."

After several minutes, the director of the meeting led Hudson gently from the stage. He was still repeating the same phrase. Perhaps he could see what lay ahead for China.

Hudson was now sixty-eight years old and badly in need of rest. Jennie made arrangements to take him to Switzerland, where the fresh air and walks in the mountains helped him to get better.

However, it was not long before telegrams began to arrive from the China Inland Mission headquarters in London. Each one seemed to bring worse news than the one before. In China, the empress dowager had declared war on foreigners, and many Chinese people had been happy to help her out. Churches were burned to the ground, and missionaries' homes looted. A missionary family were killed in their beds; others were fleeing for their lives. Hudson was shocked. They were his beloved people, and he was too far away to help. As the telegrams piled up on the table, he told Jennie, "I cannot read, I cannot think, I cannot even pray; but I can trust."

Thousands of Chinese Christians, called "secondary devils," were also being killed because they were seen as traitors to China. In Peking alone, fifteen to twenty thousand Chinese Catholics were killed. Those were black days for China.

By the time the Boxer Uprising had been defeated, one hundred thirty Protestant missionaries and over fifty of their children had been killed. The China Inland Mission alone lost fifty-eight missionaries and twenty-one children. Hudson wept for every one of them.

Hudson could only think back to the first days when he had fought so hard not to start a missionary organization, and how he had finally come to understand that each person who was called was in God's care. He could do no more than to pray for each of the dead missionaries' families.

Slowly, the mission, and Hudson, began to recover from all the horrible deaths. Hudson and Jennie took long walks in the mountains together. They befriended counts and countesses, peasants and storekeepers. Visitors flooded in from around the world, leaving some to laugh and shake their heads. The Taylors had made a China Inland Mission outpost halfway up a mountain in Switzerland.

A year went by. Hudson read his Bible through for the fortieth time. He wrote hundreds of letters and prayed constantly for China and the missionaries who served there. The news that Jennie had cancer hardly changed their lives at all. Both of them were already living in the light of eternity. Although she was thin and weak, she told a friend, "I couldn't be better cared for or happier. I'm nearly home. What will it be to be there! The Lord is taking me slowly and gently." And so He was. On July 29, 1904, Jennie died with Hudson at her bedside.

Hudson was now seventy-two years old and badly wanted to go back to China. There were so many people to encourage there and so many people to thank. So, in the spring of 1905, he and his son Howard, now also a medical doctor, and Howard's wife, Geraldine, set off on Hudson's eleventh journey to China.

And what a trip it was. Hudson was able to visit many areas by train now. Trains were much more comfortable than the wheelbarrows he used to ride in. Everywhere he went, people gathered to listen to him. He had his seventy-third birthday at one of the seven China Inland Mission stations in Henan Province. The Chinese Christians made him a huge, red satin banner which read, "O man greatly beloved."

Hudson visited China Inland Mission hospitals and orphanages, new mission stations, and the home in Yang-chow where he and Maria had survived the riot. He also visited the cemetery where Maria, Grace, Samuel, Noel, and his adult daughter Maria were all buried.

Later that day, he spoke to a new group of missionaries with China Inland Mission who were about to go into the interior. He looked at these young people who had left their families and friends to take the Gospel message to the Chinese people, and for a moment he was one of them: a twenty-one-year-old landing in China with no money, no wife, and no plan. Yet, he had trusted God, and God had used him. Now, fifty-four years later, over eighteen thousand Chinese Christians had been baptized, and the China Inland Mission had eight hundred twenty-five missionaries.

"It's a great privilege to meet you here," he told the group. "I have met many here in days gone by. My dear wife died by me here. In spirit our loved ones may be nearer to us than we think; and God is near, nearer than we think."

And Hudson was nearer to his loved ones than anyone might have imagined. On June 3, 1905, several weeks after visiting the graves of his family, Hudson Taylor died quietly in his bed. He was buried beside Maria and his children. His tombstone read: "Hudson Taylor, a man in Christ." His life had ended where he had always wanted to be: deep in the heart of China.

Steer, Roger. *Hudson Taylor: Lessons in Discipleship.* Monarch Publications, 1995.

Steer, Roger. *J. Hudson Taylor: A Man in Christ.* OMF Books, 1993.

Thompson, Phyllis. *God's Adventurer.* OMF Books, 1994.

Taylor, Dr. and Mrs. Howard. *Hudson Taylor in Early Years: The Growth of a Soul.* OMF Books, 1988 edition.

Taylor, Dr. and Mrs. Howard. *Hudson Taylor and the China Inland Mission: The Growth of a Work of God.* OMF Books, 1988 edition.

Taylor, J. Hudson. *Hudson Taylor.* Bethany House Publishers.

Janet and Geoff Benge are a husband and wife writing team with more than thirty years of writing experience. Janet is a former elementary school teacher. Geoff holds a degree in history. Originally from New Zealand, the Benges spent ten years serving with Youth With A Mission. They have two daughters, Laura and Shannon, and an adopted son, Lito. They make their home in the Orlando, Florida, area.

CHRISTIAN HEROES: THEN & NOW are available in paperback, e-book, and audiobook formats, with more coming soon!

www.HeroesThenAndNow.com